THE BLACK LIST

THE BLACK LIST

CK

TIMOTHY GREENFIELD-SANDERS
ELVIS MITCHELL

ATRIA BOOKS
New York   London   Toronto   Sydney

ATRIA
BOOKS

A Division of Simon & Schuster, Inc.
1230 Avenue of the Americas
New York, NY 10020

First Atria Books hardcover edition September 2008

ATRIA BOOKS and colophon are trademarks
of Simon & Schuster, Inc.

For information about special discounts for bulk
purchases, please contact Simon & Schuster
Special Sales at 1-800-456-6798 or
business@simonandschuster.com.

Designed by Nancy Singer

Manufactured in the United States of America

10 9 8 7 6 5 4 3 2 1

Library of Congress Cataloging-in-Publication Data

Timothy Greenfield-Sanders.
  The Black list / Timothy Greenfield-Sanders and Elvis Mitchell.—
1st Atria Books hardcover ed.
    p. cm.
1. African-Americans—Biography. 2. Celebrities—United
States—Biography. 3. African-Americans—Social
conditions—1975– 4. African-Americans—Social life and
customs. 5. African-Americans—Intellectual life. 6. African-
American arts. 7. United States—Race relations. 8. United
States—Social life and customs. 9. United States—Intellectual
life. I. Elvis Mitchell. II. Title.

E185.96.M55 2008
920'.009296073—dc22   2008015381

ISBN-13: 978-1-4165-9419-2
ISBN-10:   1-4165-9419-1

LIST

CONTENTS

INTRODUCTION

by Elvis Mitchell

What is a Black List? Historically, Americans know exactly what it is: a group of people punished by being marginalized and denied work or social approval, generally for their having taken political stands. And, for African-Americans, it's yet another slap at the word *black,* which includes such slurs as *black sheep* and *blackguard*. *The Simpsons Movie* cleverly takes aim at the tired attitude toward black when Mayor Quimby is forced to deal with an emergency by declaring "code black," and Lenny groans, "Black? That's the worst color!" Another Clinton—George, Parliament-Funkadelic founder—bounced the taint when he proclaimed in song that he wanted to "Paint the White House Black."

With the serious attention directed at Senator Barack Obama's 2008 presidential campaign, the concept doesn't seem as much like the dance floor science fiction that Dr. Funkenstein chuckled his way through. Although the creakily derogatory stamp on the word *black* predates creation of these United States, the negative connotation is the reason why, until the 1960s, respectable people of color didn't want to be called black; it was nothing short of an insult. Not until race pride shocked the country out of its ignoring and ignorant attitudes about the impact of, well, blacks on America, did the word take on a fresher and desirable aspect for many African-Americans, especially the young; the Afrocentric revolutionaries and the integrationist civil rights workers alike found something desirable about being known as black. For years before the 1960s, of course, it had the transgressive allure of cool. An underground recycling of the concept

1

was taking place—in those halcyon days before cable TV, the internet, and bar codes burned onto youth culture so that its shopping habits could be tracked and exploited—in the shady bunkers beneath the Establishment, where jazz and blues musicians plied their trade for an appreciative audience of freethinkers who were disinclined to be described as Negroes, the verbal equivalent of a pat on the head and a five-cent tip.

For me, the real question is, What's in a Black List? All of those past associations, as grim and lethal as an undertow, are to be obliterated by the new implications of the term that we're creating here. Timothy Greenfield-

Sanders and I decided that *The Black List* would be made up of portraits in both senses of the word: pictorial and verbal. What I didn't realize until we undertook the Black List is our essential similarity of interest; we are both primarily curious and pointed toward finding ways to get people to reveal themselves—he with his camera, and me through questions. The results that we managed for *The Black List* come from the living-portraiture approach, done with a formality and familiarity that I think is rare and thrilling. The subjects reacted to this technique with a confidence born of esteem for every part of their lives, rather than just their areas of endeavor or expertise. The relationship is seen in Kareem Abdul-Jabbar's smiling as he talks in depth about Harlem, Miles Davis, and his fascination with American history, as well as his days on the basketball court for UCLA, Milwaukee, and the Lakers.

Here, the term Black List becomes a reboot, a gathering of some of the most capable and, just as important, determined African-Americans, whose work and careers leave a trail of inspiration in fields ranging from politics and letters to civil rights and corporate responsibility. What they all have in common is a kind of activism, furthering the cause of African-American visibility while not shirking devotion to family and morality; that tradition of "each one teach one," and elevating the race—watchwords that still have import for much of black American society as the gap between the well-off and the black citizenry left behind mired in deprivation grows wider. For me it's a rescue that complements the world that I've grown up in, something that blacks raised in this land hear one way or another at one point or another.

2

So much of African-American cultural history is about reclamation. That understanding that nothing should be thrown out reminds me of something my Mississippi-born-and-bred grandmother said to me when I noticed so many pork products—headcheese, pigs' feet—pickling in jars in her kitchen that I half expected Boris Karloff to pull a lever, and a bolt of revivifying lightning shock them back to life: "Baby, we eat everything on the pig but the oink." Frankly, the oink sounded like a less scary—and less smelly—prospect for a meal than the chitlins that boiled away for what seemed like my entire childhood on her stove. But her words have sat with me for the rest of my life, and revisit me on occasions such as sitting in an Italian restaurant when a dollop of lardo is offered as a spread. It would never occur to me to wrinkle my nose at it; I grew up on what were the discards and what are now found in the pricier establishments around the globe. (Other words of my grandmother's come to mind: "Honey, the wheel turn slowly, but it turn.")

One of the purposes of this Black List is to track the black experience in America, and by doing so, to exhibit the wealth of variety in it. What's evident from the speakers on the Black List is how that experience defies definition. Vernon Jordan puts it as simply as saying that African-American thought is not monolithic. Women's rights crusader Faye Wattleton voices the idea that integration has caused problems as well as solved them; the areas that once housed every layer of the African-American social strata, from professionals to laborers, clergy to philosophers, offered illustrations of virtue to all within hailing distance; once those restrictions that kept blacks together were removed, a whole class of people was left behind without models next door to follow through the corridors of attainment. The necessity of having examples literally within reach is not lost on her. For those pursuing art, avoiding the simplistic classifications of blackness is a full-time occupation itself; dancer-choreographer Bill T. Jones discusses the limitations of the cliché of black rage, and the dangers of not acknowledging his blackness first and foremost—which for him was an aesthetic self-abnegation but which his detractors saw as renunciation and selling out. Dealing with blackness for others is a call to arms; Pulitzer Prize–winning playwright Suzan-Lori Parks embraces what might be called the nontraditional behavior of black audiences by providing context for it and looking to incorporate these responses into her work.

The journeys taken by Jones and Parks, as well as others here, are reflections of what blacks in America have always had to do: make their way in the world and comment on the repression as it happens, using irony as well as persistence to keep moving forward. Keenen Ivory Wayans speaks of his breakthrough film, *Hollywood Shuffle,* and television comedy, *In Living Color,* which served both those purposes. He brought his understanding of what was missing from the mainstream; the kinds of things discussed among blacks but never portrayed in movies, like the depiction of black fear (not the stuff of racist Hollywood movies of the 1930s and 1940s, in which African-Americans were reduced to cowardly stereotypes).

The sheer force of will required to be a success while being condescended to (under the best of circumstances) is frequently in evidence; condescension must have felt like a constant greeting to the subjects found on this Black List. Negro League baseball star Mahlon Duckett refuses to wallow in what might have been; self-pity would be an unwelcome distraction from his pursuit of excellence and the education he got seeing Major League players up close and finding that they weren't any better than his colleagues laboring under a system that didn't allow for adequate stats for black players. Studio Museum of Harlem chief curator Thelma Golden takes it in stride, and any hint of dismissal lights a fire under her. For Vernon Jordan, it's the example set in his neighborhood by the educated blacks whose pride in accomplishment adds a bounce to their walk as they pass by him.

One way or another, the constant reminder of being black is always close at hand; for Slash, the specter of responsibility rises when his then partner in Guns N' Roses, singer Axl Rose, spews an ugly mouthful of venom at a group of targets that includes "niggers" with the song "One in a Million," and the guitarist who rarely had race mentioned in his presence is suddenly the target of anger by blacks who demand that he take a stand. What's most powerful about the incident is how the hot splash of Rose's hatefulness lingers in Slash's soul long after he's forgotten the specifics of Axl's lyrics. (You can't help but wonder if purging the words from his mind was his way of rejecting Rose's cruelty.)

Nowhere does the boldness of converting offal into something to be proud of come more into play than language. Consider the 1980s, when the word *nigger* was pried loose from the jaws of racists and given new weight by rappers. Russell Simmons and Steve Stoute discuss the momentum and tragedy that this new stream of black consciousness evokes. Rap flourished during a crucial period in which the lag time between information spilling from the black underground into the mainstream was shortened from weeks or even years into mere moments, and the gravitational pull of black culture could no longer be denied, let alone fought. Whites barely had time to register what was being said before something was added to the rap glossary, its insistent reinvention provoking as much fear as excitement. Simmons and Stoute address this phenomenon as well with concise observations.

It was about this period, as I was interviewing a prominent black entertainer, that I mentioned snatching the word *blacklist* out of its toxic ditch. He told me that a friend of his coined "Black Pack" as a spin on a term then used to describe a group of celebrities: "Brat Pack." I said that, as a kid, I'd always imagined it was a cool thing until I had its history explained to me in school. And my friends used it as a down-low category to compile names of black people whose achievements meant something to us, such as the women authors whose fiction was collected in the book *Black-Eyed Susans and Midnight Birds* (where I first read Toni Morrison, who appears in the gallery of notables assembled for this edition). Some part of me always imagined that James Brown was only a heartbeat away from releasing an album titled *The Black List,* in which he'd put together a gaggle of the elements of African-American culture that most influenced him. As Brown's protégé Al Sharpton mentions in his section, Brown made American culture black by sweating out his own beat for the whole country—and eventually the world—rather than diluting his message and driving for audiences, as crossover performers before him had done. And because of his example, black culture crossed over in the mainstream forever. Sharpton also adds his feelings about rap and the damage he feels it has left.

Black culture existed as a code; notes from underground. The spirituals were delivered from the gospel as encoded messages from the slaves, so that escapes could be plotted, and missives were songs as information, so that it was known when the overseers and masters were about. That underground still exists for black artists. Zane crafted her fiction solely for her own self-expression and posted it online, to find that an audience hungry for her combination of erotica and self-examination existed and clamored for more of the dialogues her characters had with each other. Even after being evicted from one website, the compulsions of her creations—and the need for black women, unused to this kind of raw honesty, to keep up with her work—continued to find a place, finally, in print.

Perhaps language and culture have come to mean so much to African-Americans because, until the last century, it was something we owned that couldn't be taken away from us. Blacks weren't allowed to own land in a great deal of the United States for most of this country's history (California had clauses preventing home ownership by African-Americans until the 1960s, for example), and the intense hold on our culture provided a spiritual home for us. Former New Orleans mayor and National Urban League President Marc Morial reminds us of the need for home, literal and metaphorical, as he summarizes black political progress—and how quickly racism can reemerge in the twenty-first century—through the microcosm of his birthplace, pre- and post–Hurricane Katrina. His thoughtfulness and carefully contained passion are valuable notes to be sounded at a time when so many want to conclude that race is no longer an issue in the United States.

African-American culture is something that we all created here together because so many blacks were stolen from their homelands, and we became the melting pot that was extolled as the motto of this country— even as so many Europeans got to cling to their respective traditions as they supposedly assimilated. Assimilation was not merely an option for African-Americans, it was a means of survival, since the only other choice was death. And the conflation of nations and peoples led to the amalgam that is now—and has been—among the most potent artistic and social exports America has created. It is a culture that includes Toni Morrison and Russell Simmons, Vernon Jordan and Thelma Golden, Susan Rice and Colin Powell, Bill T. Jones and Dawn Staley, Slash and Zane. In Ralph Ellison's introduction to *Invisible Man,* the title character keeps reciting a refrain from a Louis Armstrong song that perpetually rolls around in his head: "What did I do to be so black and blue?" The blues that each of the subjects in the Black List endured aren't limned from the poetry of suffering, they are the hues of bruises, the marks gained from stepping into the fray and coming out bloody but unbowed; each warrior is happy to explain the stories behind all of the scars and lacerations. No one holds anything back, and part of the pleasure I got from listening to all of them was watching as their guards dropped and they opened up in front of Timothy's camera. And if you, the reader, get a glimmer of the exhilaration I felt as each of the figures here spoke at length about their wishes, their battles, their anxieties, and fulfilling their goals while getting through the everyday vagaries of life, then that imparts an extra sweetness to victory.

Go through this new-century version of a blacklist; I think your perceptions of it, and of Black America, will be changed forever in the same ways that Timothy's and mine were. No doubt, the word *black* has outgrown much of the downbeat past, and all it took was several hundred years and a different kind of home-style thoughtfulness: black American ingenuity, which is as much about reinvention as it is invention. That's the heart of the Black List that will carry us forward.

SLASH

GUITARIST

SONGWRITER

MY MOM HAD really eclectic taste in music. It went anywhere from Led Zeppelin to James Brown to Minnie Riperton to Funkadelic. At a young age, I knew what I liked and what I didn't like. And obviously the stuff that I liked, I was really in touch with. I think it was my grandmother who turned me on to stuff like Elmore James and B. B. King and Albert King. I just picked up on the stuff that was the most soulful. Not that

Los Angeles, October 23, 2007

my grandmother was just a blues nut sitting around listening to blues greats. But somewhere in there, there was a lot of blues stuff going on because she was very familiar with it. So, I guess it was just without me consciously knowing what was going on. Or being able to pick one genre from the next as far as types of music were concerned. I ended up just listening to Albert King stuff all the time. When I was probably, like, seven, eight, nine, ten years old, I used to hang out over at my aunt Johnny's place, which is basically, you know, South Central L.A. and that's where my cousins on my mom's side, Wayne and Edward, lived. They could both play. They would just naturally pick up a bass and drums and just play, not knowing what they were doing. And they were amazing. And so once I'd picked up guitar, by the time I was fifteen, I would go over there, and I would jam with those guys.

I WAS NEVER REALLY FAZED BY THE COLOR BARRIER.

I was never really fazed by the color barrier. I think my mom paid more attention to it than I did. Because, you know, she grew up in a time when there was definitely a lot of discrimination going on. Ignorance is bliss in some ways. I just never paid that much attention to it. And I wasn't confronted too much with it on the street. I mean, there was the occasional thing. I obviously wasn't all the way black, and I wasn't all the way white. I was sort of stuck somewhere in the middle. I was sort of always an outcast in everything anyway. People I don't know ask me, "So, where are you from? You know, what's your background? What's your origin?" They usually think I'm either Latino or this or that or the other. But on the professional level, I think it's pretty common knowledge that I'm half black or whatever. But then there's this infamous Jewish rumor about me as well; I'm in the Jewish book of famous people.

I think the only time there was a realization of the ethnic difference between myself and Axl was when we put out this song called "One in a Million," which he wrote. That was the first time that I was, like, "You know, I don't really feel comfortable with you making these statements in this particular song." We fought about it. And it ended up coming out anyway. And then the fact that I was black became very apparent to people on the street. You know, a lot of black dudes would come up and go, "Why did you allow that to happen?" And I'd have to explain that to 'em. I think the lyrics in it were—I can't even remember—"Immigrants and faggots and police and niggers."

With Jimi Hendrix, I think the thing that set him aside from the other guitar players, his peers at the time, was that he was so established in expressing himself on a level that most people were merely just playing the guitar, putting chords together and some notes that go along, and it's all very nice. What he was doing was strangling the guitar and making things come out of it that you wouldn't really expect out of a piece of maple with six strings on it. It was otherworldly. All things considered, I think that once Jimi became as big as he became, anybody who was trying to keep him down back in the beginning had to change their tune a little bit. The Jimi Hendrix thing is actually really interesting. But, the funny thing about white music, especially in rock, was that it was all influenced by black musicians.

But nobody really accepted that. So when Jimi came out and played what they used to call "acid rock," he was really bridging that gap. And you know, blacks weren't really totally ready for that. They weren't ready to accept that. I think one of the reasons why Jimi was such a huge crossover success is because all the British guys were so influenced by black musicians. Jimi came along and really, you know, right in front of them was able to take the music that was so popular at that particular time and bring this element to it which is uniquely black.

The weird thing about the rock and roll press is that they can never identify that stuff. "Sweet Child O' Mine," when we actually recorded that song, the guitar solos for that piece, I don't even know where that comes from, because I wasn't consciously in tune with Albert King at that point. At that point there were a lot of guitar players that I'd been influenced by. But they were the next generation up. And it turns out that all those guitar players were influenced by Albert King and a ton of other guitar players from way back in the day. But I wasn't really hip to that then. Because by the time we'd done "Sweet Child O' Mine," I'd only been playing for about four or five years. And I didn't really know that much. So, that was really just spontaneous guitar playing. Just the way that I played not knowing where the influences really came from. I started to really understand where my style comes from as I got a little bit older and had been playing a little longer.

There was a moment that happened about three years ago. I went into a restaurant, and a middle-aged black lady came up and asked for my autograph. Right? She's probably late forties, early fifties. And I was like, "Okay." And she pulled out of her purse the Guns N' Roses greatest hits album. And I was like, "You happen to have that on you?" "I just bought it." "Wow." That was a moment for me. That's when I realized that you know, despite all that pissing and moaning about whatever was pissing us off at the time, I'm still really proud of it. Because we kept our attitude intact. But it was interesting to see it become so hugely successful.

I got a phone call from my manager saying, "Michael Jackson's trying to get in touch with you." And I was pretty starstruck. You know, it's like,

"Really?" In a way, you get that feeling of "I guess I have arrived." He called me up, and it was *that voice* on the other end of the phone. And he said, "I'd like you to play on my record," you know? And so I was, like, "OK." I went down to the Record Plant in L.A., and I met him there. And he was with his date at the time, Brooke Shields, right? And he just said, "Nice to meet you. This is Brooke. We're gonna go to dinner." And he just left me with the music. I had pretty much free rein to do whatever it was that I wanted with the music they gave me. And he did his thing.

I had one band called Snakepit. I hired this singer who was from Virginia. His name was Rod Jackson and he is one of the most awesome vocalists I've heard since I've been around. He's a black guy with a pretty, you know, sort of old-school soul kind of voice. I signed him on to do Snakepit. As soon as I turned in the material to—I think it was Interscope—Jimmy Iovine, he was like, "Oh, we love it. But we're not sure about the singer." And I really got this feeling that they didn't relate to the sort of heavy rock-and-roll kind of thing. Sort of almost a heavy-metal kind of musical vibe mixed with that kind of soulful voice, which I thought was perfect. They couldn't relate to it at all. People, by and large—in this industry especially—still and I think always will have a hard time trying to put aside the stereotypes and just listen to things for what they are. It's always gonna take some maverick and individual to be able to put out something that people aren't expecting.

When N.W.A. and 2 Live Crew were big, that was right around the same time that Guns N' Roses was coming together. So those were our two favorite bands. Because that was the shit. You know, if you wanted hard-edged, urban music, that was it. I remember we listened to that stuff constantly. I think it's been really diluted since then. But Guns N' Roses was the antithesis of everything that was going on at that point, you know?

PEOPLE, BY AND LARGE—IN THIS INDUSTRY ESPECIALLY—STILL AND I THINK ALWAYS WILL HAVE A HARD TIME TRYING TO PUT ASIDE THE STEREOTYPES AND JUST LISTEN TO THINGS FOR WHAT THEY ARE.

SLASH

TONI MORRISON

NOVELIST

PROFESSOR

NOBEL LAUREATE

I WAS LUCKY because when I received the information about having won the Nobel Prize for Literature, I was very deep into writing *Paradise*. So I did not have that creative problem of now that you've won the Nobel Prize, what are you going to do? Writing for me is the only free place. It's the only place where I'm not doing what

New York City, February 8, 2007

somebody else wants or asks or needs. Writing is mine. So there are no critics in there. There are no reviewers in there. And that's so important to me. Because it demands a kind of authenticity and honesty that nothing else does. So winning the Nobel Prize, suddenly I am in a different league.

At some point, the most incredible thing to me was how in at least one major newspaper and maybe others, my having won the Nobel Prize was understood to be controversial. Journalists ran around and phoned people who thought it was controversial. Racially controversial. Or in terms of quality. And that's what they wrote about. Not about the fact that an American and a woman had won, as though that was, you know, irrelevant. It's just that there was some negative controversial part, the tendency on the part of some people to reduce much of the work that I had done. To just make it simple and flat and cartoonish was overwhelming in some places. I had to trust my own judgment and my own abilities, and also trust the judgment of people who didn't read that way—who weren't looking for some reason to despise the effort. You know, some personal reason to make sure that it was not read properly. As for the rest of my life really nothing changed, except that I sometimes had to make other people feel comfortable around me. Or do something with my eyes to make them feel comfortable. I didn't have to do that before. Now I sort of have to. And then they would calm down right away.

> WRITING FOR ME IS THE ONLY FREE PLACE. IT'S THE ONLY PLACE WHERE I'M NOT DOING WHAT SOMEBODY ELSE WANTS OR ASKS OR NEEDS.

Frederick Douglass, et cetera, is the classic black slave story. Bondage. Escape. Freedom. One thing that was not part of the slave story was a woman: escaped or not escaped. What was going on in an interior way with women who got out, or who were taken out, or who were run out. So that was my effort in writing *Beloved,* to do that. To talk about a woman who had to make some choices about slavery. About motherhood. About love. About parenting. About all sorts of things. That was a complicated story. It had nothing to do with being a victim. It had something to do with trying to deal with this incredibly complicated, desperate world of a woman, like that woman, a real woman. A historical figure, as a matter of fact, who was anything but a victim. This is a woman who said, "These children are mine. I can do with them what I want."

My understanding of a powerful black woman is a little different from, I think, the contemporary one. Because my recollection of stories, tales, events, anecdotes in my family was that everybody was so badly oppressed, they did not have time for gender games. Those women had to get to the end of the row of cotton the same time or faster than the men. And everybody benefited from excellent or quick work. They were building something. So even in my own childhood, if my father came home from his work at a steel mill at three, he would babysit us. Now, it was true that later, after the war, my father said, "I do not want my wife to work."

My grandmother left her little piece of land when her husband had gone to a big city to play the violin and pick up some money. She was by herself with her six children. And she said that white boys began to circle that farm, so she had to get out. Her girls were, like, eleven, some of them, twelve, thirteen. She got her little laundry money together. I think she said thirty

dollars savings. She had a friend take them to the train station, and she sent a message to her husband that says we're on XYZ train. Meet us. Going north. Don't know where. We're getting out. And he was there. I mean, he didn't come on right away. He hid. Because he thought that they were in debt. Sharecroppers, whatever. And she still did womanly things. She cooked, she sewed. But there was no fight about that. Because the bigger fight was life, food, you

know, let's get on. Then when you get a little luxury, you begin to decide or believe that there are female jobs and male jobs, et cetera, et cetera, et cetera. So I didn't feel the threat of being a woman who could take charge as much as I could of my life. I was encouraged by my father to think that way.

He thought I was the smartest thing in the world, my sister and I. He thought we were lovely. And funny. And sort of charming—but tough. As a young girl, twelve years old, I'm working in somebody's kitchen a couple of hours after school. Feeling very lucky about that two dollars a week. But I don't know what I'm doing. The woman has equipment I never saw before. She would complain. So I would come home and complain. And my mother's response was, "Well, then quit." I couldn't do that because it's two dollars, right?

I complained to my father. And he says, "You don't live there. You live here with your people. Go to work, get your money, and come on home." And

TONI MORRISON

he took pride in good work, you know. It's a very important thing to be told at that age what your talents are.

My older sister got married when she graduated from high school. She wanted very much to get married then. She didn't want to go to college. I did. So I went to college. And my father was very proud of that. And my mother was very proud of that.

They promised me they could do it for a year. They said, "We only have enough money to do it for one." "I only need one," I said. Then I learned that among white girls of a certain age, that was not common; white families educated the boys and not the girls. But it was entirely different in the black community. The fathers pushed the girls to go to college. The mothers pushed the girls to go to college even if they couldn't send the sons. Because the girls—if they went away—could get nurturing jobs: teachers, nurses, some nonthreatening thing.

If black families pushed their men, their boys, they would want to be promoted. They would be in a rivalry and confrontational situation. So that's like the race itself decided how to survive and reproduce itself in levels. So you have families in which all the girls are educated and not the boys. And

what I remember was that there was no contest about that. The brothers were pleased that this was happening. It was about trying to get out of an economically depressed situation. So with all of that in my head as kind of taken for granted, I had no fear of men. Because the most important man in my life was my father. I took that with me.

And when I got into difficult situations working in an institution in which the people who judged me were those people, it never occurred to me that I was only worth what they said. I just never thought that. They did evaluate me, you know, in terms of raises, et cetera. But I never thought that was true. That was just the way it was. And I always thought that I was head of a household just like they were. That was what I demanded for myself. I didn't always get it, but it's like any other negotiation. If you do that, you have to be willing to quit. You have to be willing to lose— really lose—if you're going to make those claims. But I was willing.

My mother talked about her dreams as though they were events. She never said, "I dreamed." And we would listen to these dreams. For her it was part of her life, you know. And at the same time, this was a woman who, when they put the eviction notices up on the wall or the door, she tore them off. If you have no access to the political life or the governmental life or the institutional life of your world, you do reinvent or invent a reliance on religion, magic—something else that's yours. So that's part of this life that is enchanted. It's an enchanted life they lead. But at the same time they really do have to get that meal and go down to the tracks. We used to go down with little bags, pick up coal that had been dropped, and bring it home to heat up the house. At the same time, there was this enchanted world that we lived in, because people talked about it as though it were enchanted. And we began to think of it that way while we were doing this very practical, no-nonsense, get-the-job-done-and-stop-whining thing.

I didn't know I had a voice until *Sula*. I mean, you don't know when you write one book if you're ever going to sound like that again. Or whether that sound was mostly for the book. But then when I began to write *Sula*, I could hear the same language, a kind of language that I liked and was natural to me to write in. Dramatic literature. All my life, it's been in those areas. Some things have just overwhelmed me, and other things not. It's a confluence. But out of that world of literature, you try to carve this mammy, whore. Those two categories are laid down for black women's representation. Almost all of the African-American women writers that I know were very much uninterested in one area: white men. So they tend not to ever write about them. They're sort of in the background somewhere. That frees up a lot. It frees up the imagination because you don't have the gaze, you know. And when I say white men, I don't mean just the character, but the establishment. The reviewers. The publishers. The people who are in control. Once you erase that from your canvas, you can really play.

TONI MORRISON

KEENEN
IVORY WAYANS

WRITER

DIRECTOR

PRODUCER

ACTOR

WHEN ROBERT TOWNSEND and I decided to do *Hollywood Shuffle,* it really was born out of frustration. We decided we would just do it on our own. It was fun because we had no idea what we were doing. And ignorance was our greatest asset—the fact that we didn't know we weren't supposed to be able to make a movie without money, without experienced people, without permits. We'd put all the equipment in a van. We'd have somebody stand on

Los Angeles, October 24, 2007

VERNON JORDAN

LAWYER

CIVIL RIGHTS ACTIVIST

PRESIDENT, NATIONAL URBAN LEAGUE,

1972–1981

I THINK I always knew my mother was the visionary. I think that had I finished high school, got a job in the post office, bought a little white house with green shutters and a white picket fence, nice wife, two children, cut my grass every week, washed my car every week, went to Sunday school, went to church, listened to the news, read the newspaper, paid my taxes, voted, my father would've said that's a very good life.

New York City, December 12, 2007

FAYE WATTLETON

PRESIDENT, CENTER FOR THE ADVANCEMENT
 OF WOMEN
PRESIDENT, PLANNED PARENTHOOD,
 1978–1992

WE AS A PEOPLE were religious speakers. And we as a people have always honored our religious leaders. They gave us a hope beyond the oppression that we endured and suffered in slavery. So when you are an oppressed people, the possibility of a hereafter, a better life, and the leaders who can help you to imagine a better life, become revered, and very important, and respected figures. That is a part of the community that has

New York City, August 8, 2007

MARC MORIAL

PRESIDENT, NATIONAL URBAN LEAGUE

MAYOR OF NEW ORLEANS, 1994–2002

at night, pull into the driveway, turn off the lights, and blow the horn so my mother could come out to just make sure that there was no one there.

For him becoming mayor in 1977 was really the capstone of a career which began in the fifties when he was a lawyer for the NAACP Legal Defense Fund alongside A. P. Toorow and Thurgood Marshall and Connie Motley. And later he became president of the NAACP branch. He became the first African-American elected to the state legislature in Louisiana since Reconstruction, first African-American judge. In many ways, his career was symbolic of the change that was taking place in the South, taking place in Louisiana, and taking place in New Orleans at that time. My father discouraged my brother and me from getting involved in politics—sort of suggested that we do other things with our lives. But growing up in a family where both my father and mother were civil rights activists—my mother was a schoolteacher and very active in the teachers' union—was, in effect, growing up in a household with a climate of giving. The climate of community service was just imbued in us. I remember going to civil rights marches at five and six and seven years old.

My father died very suddenly in 1989. He had been out of office three years. At the time he died, we were contemplating practicing law together. He had left the mayor's office and had joined a law firm. And we were beginning to talk about how maybe we were at a point in life where we ought to try to practice together. His death, I think, compelled me to want to serve the public in an elected position. It encouraged me. My father was only sixty years of age, still very youthful, still very energetic, with so much to contribute.

> MY FATHER DISCOURAGED MY BROTHER AND ME FROM GETTING INVOLVED IN POLITICS—SORT OF SUGGESTED THAT WE DO OTHER THINGS WITH OUR LIVES.

I think that a number of my siblings are not political in the sense of not wanting to be in the public eye. And at times my career in the public eye may have caused discomfort for them. Sometimes it causes people to want to intrude into your privacy, be curious about what you're doing, and not recognize that in my family I have a sister who is a lawyer. I have a sister who is a doctor. I have a sister who is a banker. I have a brother who's been an investment banker and a community activist and has done a number of things. And all of my siblings have college degrees and graduate school degrees and careers of their own. And when one sibling is in public office or in the public eye there is probably also some pain. People who choose not to be in the public eye, and wanna be private with their children and with their affairs and with what they do, sometimes don't appreciate newspapers being curious about what they're doing. People in the community wondering what they're up to. Two of my sisters while I was mayor did not live in the city, for the most part.

New Orleans is a classic case of a tale of two cities. The underbelly of New Orleans is a city that has struggled with great racial and economic divisions. A city where there's a high degree of poverty. And there is a built-in class, if you will, an old-guard economic elite that has historically resisted change. They've resisted change because they've sought to retain their position of authority and power. And in my view, that old economic guard has been the primary force in holding back the transformation of the city. What makes New Orleans unique among the Southern cities is that great, great battle between tradition and progress. Which continues to this very day. One thing I would add—and this is an important historic perspective—is that the early New Orleans of the 1700s and the early 1800s had a substantial black population. So African-Americans and their history is intertwined with everything New Orleans is. Wynton Marsalis says New Orleans is the only city in the world with its own culture, its own language, its own music, its own way of doing things.

You know, I think what the jury's still out on is the question of why those flood walls along those canals broke. And I think that it is only when the many, many lawsuits that have been filed against the Army Corps get to court, and some light is shed on the decision-making process for the construction of those levees that people will really know why there were four or five levee breaks in the days following Katrina. Everyone in my family had water of some level in their homes. When you step away from it, the most important thing is that your family members survived. I have so many friends who lost family members. And then friends whose family members have not been able to survive the aftermath of the storm: the stress, the pressure, the depression, the trauma, the sense of being uprooted and living in a strange city, in a strange place for a number of months or even a year. America remains a tale of two cities. What Katrina did was to put it out

MARC MORIAL

so people could see it. And while some people criticized the media, I don't criticize the media. 'Cause all they did was turn on their cameras.

Katrina is an American tragedy. It should never be forgotten. How the old economic guard could be so intent on trying to turn the hands of time back in the city—it's as though certain people, after the hurricane, cheered that a lot of African-Americans were displaced. You know, the cocktail commentary was, "Good. These folks are gone. We will rebuild the city without them." It was hard-hearted. And in my view, the division is one of the things that has stymied the recovery. A house divided cannot stand. And a house divided cannot move. And for New Orleans to move forward, it cannot be a house divided. It has to be a house unified. I saw so many things I didn't understand. And I asked myself, "Is this the city I know and love?" I was very impacted by the events of 9/11. And I asked myself when Katrina was going on, "Is this the city I know? And why can't the nation follow the model of 9/11 when it comes to Katrina?"

You know, what happened in Katrina rocked my confidence in my own government. It didn't shatter it, but it rocked it. I just felt that even if

the initial response was wobbly, at some point you right the ship. And you ensure that everything from that point is going to be done to the highest of standards. And I think that what's happened here is that the people around the president, the people around the governor, the people around the mayor, have felt that pointing fingers is better than working together and getting something done.

During 9/11 I happened to be President of the United States Conference of Mayors. I had a national platform. And I had an opportunity to be a participant in the effort that was under way at that time to unify, for people to understand that the attack affected people of all backgrounds and races. There was no sense from the leadership which said, "You know what? Everyone has suffered. So we've all suffered." And there needed to be that kind of leadership, particularly from local leaders. Too much of the local leadership at that point was a struggle over who would control the future destiny of the city. And it turned into just a confluence of confusion over what the plan would be, over what the direction of the city would be.

I remember as a child traveling to the East Coast with my father and mother to New York and Philadelphia and Washington and Boston. And from the time I was a child it was like this is where you want to go to college, where you want to go have this experience outside of New Orleans. And I think going away changed me in a lot of ways. Because what it helped me to see is that New Orleans is a great city, my hometown. And so the experience of being at the University of Pennsylvania, living on the East Coast, having summer jobs in Washington, in New York, and then ultimately going to Georgetown University Law School really broadened my perspective and helped me understand my own hometown better. And is really one of the things that spurred me to want to go back and work to change New Orleans, to work to transform New Orleans.

AMERICA REMAINS A TALE OF TWO CITIES. WHAT KATRINA DID WAS TO PUT IT OUT SO PEOPLE COULD SEE IT.

MARC MORIAL

SERENA WILLIAMS

PROFESSIONAL TENNIS PLAYER

EIGHT-TIME GRAND SLAM WINNER

VENUS DEFINITELY OPENED a lot of doors for me because she was first. And she had to go through a lot of stuff that I don't even know if she talks about. You know, for me, it was like the Red Sea. She parted it and I just kinda walked through. And she made so many different opportunities available for me. I go to her for everything. And she knows every player like the back of her hand. I go to her for advice. She doesn't get any credit on

Los Angeles, March 21, 2008

how smart she is on the court. I'll be like, "OK, Venus. I'm playing so-and-so." "Hit to her backhand. And then hit a slice and come in. And all you have to do is put it away." She is really strategic on the court. And it's good, because I can pick her brain and learn a little bit. She's not my favorite opponent to play. She has the biggest serve. She runs the fastest. She gets everything back. So, who wants to play the best player? I don't.

I loved Muhammad Ali. I loved what he stood for. He even went to jail for his belief. And I think that's the ultimate role model. I mean, you can't get better than that. I don't always say what's on my mind, but I do stand up for what I believe in. My hero—tenniswise—was, obviously, Zina Garrison. I thought she was awesome. I was too young for Arthur Ashe and Althea Gibson. Zina Garrison was the greatest. I remember when I must have been like eight, we went to Texas to hit with her and Lori McNeil. My experience with Arthur Ashe was we went to a clinic that he was doing. I just remember he hit with us for a little bit. And he talked to the kids. And I was one of the kids. And I just was like, "Oh, this is so cool." I was so young, I don't remember much outside of that. I remember thinking, "Wow, I just want to shake his hand." Because, I mean, come on, he was Arthur Ashe.

I am a complete hip-hop girl. With the style, in bringing the fashion on the courts, I definitely brought kind of like a hip-hop feel to it, a young feel, getting the urban crowd into it. It's amazing the influence that black people and urban market have had on the whole world. "Bling-bling" is now in Webster's Dictionary.

I'm making an impact? I don't think about it like that. Granted, I can totally see how players are playing harder. Moving faster, running faster, and jumping higher. So I feel like I'm definitely a part of that reason, myself and my sister. Because they had to improve in order to keep competing. I always loved being who I am. And I'm never gonna change that for anyone or anything. I have to give the credit to my mom for that. She wanted all us girls to be strong black women and not to let anyone run over us in any way, shape, or form. And my mom is the ultimate strong woman. She definitely taught us to have confidence.

I think I said once, "I am the most underestimated eight-time Grand Slam champion ever." I think a lot of people got a lot of laughs out of that. I never get credit for my strategy. Every article that I do read, it's like, "She

I ALWAYS LOVED BEING WHO I AM. AND I'M NEVER GONNA CHANGE THAT FOR ANYONE OR ANYTHING.

overpowered her opponent." Which, granted, may be true. But at the same time, it's a lot more than just hitting the ball as hard as you can. My dad always said to be proactive, not reactive. I get frustrated, because they'll say another girl who's white has all this strategy. I never get credit for mental. But at the end of the day, I am very happy with me. You can't be number one or the best in tennis with just hitting hard. I actually don't believe I hit hard,

to be honest. I mean, if I get angry, then I'll hit a ball as hard as I can. But other than that, it's all about strategy and moving your opponent.

My dad is a genius coach. He taught himself tennis. He decided, one day, he wanted to learn. He taught my mom. And then they taught us. And he wasn't a spring chicken when he taught himself. And he's so innovative. He had us doing things that people are just now doing. If I'd listened better, I would probably have more Grand Slams right now. It's hard to be a parent and a coach. My mom, you know, she's a mom and a coach, which probably is even harder. I think they do a great job with it.

I've had a few experiences with being black in tennis. You would see a Lindsay Davenport playing another player from the United States. And all these people clap for her. Then, I would be playing someone from Japan. And everyone's clapping for the Japanese girl. I'm thinking, "Wait a second. Aren't I American? You know, why aren't you cheering for me?" It's something I've grown used to, though. And it's really sad. One of my favorite places to play is South Carolina. The first time I went there, people started clapping for me; I got so nervous. I just wasn't used to it. I was just so used to people rooting against me. And I lost. But that's because I just was like, "Oh, my God. This is weird. I need to hear people booing. Or I need to hear people clapping against me. Because I'm not used to it."

One of the greatest examples of racism was when I was playing in Indian Wells. I was nineteen. And I was playing Kim Clijsters, from Belgium. I walked out on the court, and everyone started booing. I mean, the whole crowd. If you know anything about Palm Springs, people go there to retire.

SERENA WILLIAMS

Everyone there, let's face it, is ninety and above. And they're all white. My dad was there, Venus was there. There weren't that many black people in the crowd. And I'm thinking, "Okay—this is strange, you know, to have a black girl playing in the midst of all these older white people." Honestly, I thought it was a joke. Then I thought maybe they were booing Kim Clijsters. Then, they made the announcements, and when they said, "Serena Williams," everyone booed. I was like, "Okay, so it is me." We're talkin' about 2001. And I'm thinking, "Wow, we're not far off the sixties, where things were segregated. So it's been forty years. It's not a long time." It was definitely, hands down, the worst experience I've ever had in tennis. They just continued to boo me. And the umpire didn't know what to do, because she'd never been in a situation like that. I talked to Kim later and she felt horrible. I was crying on the court. I didn't understand what I had done wrong. I don't know how I won the match. No, I do know. I went on the sidelines and I said a prayer. I said, "God, dear Jehovah, God, don't let me win. Just let me stay out here and just deal with this. And then have my head high." Then I went out and I won. You know, usually when you win a big tournament, you're really, really happy. But no, I was crying. And they had the nerve to want to know if I'm coming back. I'm like, "Please. Why would I go back? No. It needs to be boycotted." There's no need for me to go; if Muhammad Ali can go to jail, I don't have to play Indian Wells.

Being an African-American, I've always wanted to go see where I'm from and go to Africa and have a chance to experience that. I'm traveling to Europe all the time. I'm traveling to Russia. Places where you can count the black people—usually it's me and my mom. And, you know, I'm in Australia and Norway. And it's just like, I'm so used to hanging out with people that aren't my color. For the first time in my life, I went to a place that everywhere, people looked like me. And it's just a different feeling. It's like, you know, everyone gets that feeling when they go to Europe. But when I first had a chance to go to Africa and actually, for once, being around people that were my color.

Oh, it was just a great thing. I can't even describe the feeling. I think everyone should have an opportunity to go. It was actually a shock for me when I went to Africa, and seeing everyone of my color. And then, I got used to it, and I was so happy to be there. And I realized why I've always wanted to go there.

IF I'D LISTENED BETTER, I WOULD PROBABLY HAVE MORE GRAND SLAMS RIGHT NOW.

SERENA WILLIAMS

LOU GOSSETT JR.

ACTOR

OSCAR WINNER, 1982

VERY FORTUNATE NEIGHBORHOOD, Coney Island, after
the Depression. It was a melting pot: predominately Jewish, but also Italian
and Irish. A smattering of African-Americans. The mothers and our grand-
mothers, they were the sentinels before the cell phones. They were in the
windows making sure that we behaved ourselves. And if our parents didn't
get home in time for dinner, I had a choice: I could go and get some gefilte

Los Angeles, September 12, 2007

fish. I could go down the street and get some corned beef and cabbage. And those friends are still my friends today. So we got insulated in an ideal kind of environment. It was not until we left there and got into the reality of the rest of the world where the racial problem existed. A lot of us, of course, gravitated to Greenwich Village 'cause that was the same society.

I was a hippie, a beatnik, a flower child, and all of that. Yeah, from 1959 to 1962, at a place called the Cafe Wha? The reason why I was down there in first place was Jean Genet's avant-garde play called *The Blacks*. It paid a hot forty-five dollars a week.

I WAS A HIPPIE, A BEATNIK, A FLOWER CHILD, AND ALL OF THAT.

It was an incredibly creative time, the time of Godfrey Cambridge, Richard Pryor, Bill Cosby, and Fred Neil, the one who wrote the theme for *Midnight Cowboy*. We opened the theater on St. Mark's Place and Second Avenue. That later became the Negro Ensemble Company. But in that original cast—I get goose pimples when I talk about it—were Roscoe Lee Browne, James Earl Jones, Cicely Tyson, Maya Angelou, Raymond St. Jacques, Godfrey Cambridge. It went on for five and a half years. And the replacements were Billy Dee Williams, Lincoln Kilpatrick. We'd go away and do a movie or a play. And the play would stop, and we'd come back and play another part. So out of that came the *Roots* people, obviously.

Soon as I left the theater, I'd go down to the Village to hang out. Everybody was down there: Toni Morrison, James Baldwin. We saw each other every night. We fought, argued, cried, loved together, and created a very strong African-American art culture, which today still survives. And then came a brilliant actor by the name of James Edwards, who played an amazing character in a film called *Home of the Brave*. He came very close to getting an Academy Award. And the scuttlebutt was that James Edwards had an affair with some Caucasian actress. I won't mention her name. Something happened in public, and that was the end of James Edwards.

I created what is called "I'm gonna give you what you want, act like you want, and I'm gonna speak like you want in order to get this job and to further my career." All the way to the Academy Award. Not because it was impossible for an African-American to win it, but my competition were two great actors. And people thought those might have been their last movies. James Mason was dying. Robert Preston was dying. So I was not prepared to get an Oscar. But it's on my shelf today. Now, when my contemporaries won the Academy Award, their careers went crazy. I didn't get a phone call for a year and a half for a job. But when I won the Oscar, I said, "Wow. Now I can do the Ashanti Empire. Wow. I can play, maybe, one of the kings of Haiti." Or I wanted to play Kwame Nkrumah. I was turned down, and I had to settle for being second best to people who never did win awards.

One of the examples that I deeply object to is whenever there's a story where African-Americans have made history in the last thirty years, nine times out of ten, those characters have been played by Caucasian actors. And the audiences around the world know all about European culture. There are three or four about the Romans, a couple of the Greeks, about the Italians, about the French, King Arthur. And these young actors get these roles that I salivate for about their culture.

A good friend of mine, the late George C. Scott, got an Oscar by playing Patton. I had three uncles in the tank battalion that Patton commandeered. Then he put them on the point of the arrow against the Panzer division. And they beat the Panzer division and cut a swath to Berlin. They rescued the Jews from Buchenwald, Auschwitz, and Dachau. Those were Patton's men. So I'm watching *Patton*, and there's only one African-American actor, and he's playing Patton's valet. And you know who that African-American actor was? James Edwards.

Oh, I was madly in love with Diana Sands. I wish she was alive now. We'd still be married. We'd have all kinds of children. But I had the hots for Diana Sands, all right? Let's be official about that one. She played my wife in *The Landlord.* Hal Ashby got to do *The Landlord* as a reward for winning the Oscar for his editing work for *In the Heat of the Night.* So me and Diana had a love scene. She was light-skinned, but she had these African lips. So we had to kiss. And we kissed the way we would do off camera. And Hal said, "Cut." He went to his first assistant, who was an African-American by the name of Kurt Baker, and he says, "How can I say this?" Kurt said, "Just say it." So Hal came up to me and Diana and says, "Let me explain the new lens." I said, "What do you mean?" "Well, you see, your eye on this new lens is gonna be at least five feet wide. And your lips and your kiss are gonna be about *this* big. So when you guys are kissin', you're gonna be all lips." I mean, we took up fifteen feet of lips up there!

LOU GOSSETT JR.

RUSSELL SIMMONS

MOGUL

FOUNDER, DEF JAM RECORDS

THE FIRST TIME I heard rap was in Charles Gallery in Harlem. And then the 371 and Disco Fever and all them places where it really emerged was my first orientation with rap. You know, anybody who had one step out of the ghetto didn't like it very much. Couldn't take it to any midtown clubs.

So it was really something. All these sophisticated clubs where you had to wear shoes, those clubs didn't like rap. And they didn't like anybody

New York City, August 14, 2007

who was associated with the rap culture. It was a ghetto culture. There was no support in the music industry. The guy who signed Kurtis Blow's "Christmas Rappin'" was a British A & R director signing for London. First time it got played on the radio was in Amsterdam. It was something that the black executives thought happened on its own. And not only did the black executives not like it, these were guys who were polished. Anybody of color who had resources didn't like rap, for the same reason they don't like it now—because it comes from a group that's mostly been marginalized. And most of the time, these people are trying to escape. So that's what makes hip-hop so special all over the world, not only in America. Poor people are rappers. And their expression, it's honesty. It's shocking sometimes the language they use. It's real language. But we try to distance ourselves from it when we get in a good space, you know. And so there's hip-hop now, reminding us of our reality, the one that we're escaping and the one that's being left behind.

ANYBODY OF COLOR WHO HAD RESOURCES DIDN'T LIKE RAP, FOR THE SAME REASON THEY DON'T LIKE IT NOW—BECAUSE IT COMES FROM A GROUP THAT'S MOSTLY BEEN MARGINALIZED.

When we produced the music, we intentionally distanced ourself from all that sounded like R & B. We made sure we never used any of it. I certainly didn't use any of the bass sounds or the drum sounds or guitar sounds—nothing that sounded like a contemporary R & B record. Because all that reminded me of the same people that didn't like us; pussy-lip niggers is what my father called them. He's a professor of black history. And that's what I used to call them all the time, too. We didn't want to be that. They don't acknowledge, you know, that the reflection of that reality is a real one. It needs to come out. They want to act as if we don't talk about it, it doesn't exist. If it doesn't come out in rap, it doesn't come out at all. If they don't say "Fuck tha Police," they will never have a dialogue between police and community.

The first artist we signed, I think it was Whodini. It was way after I'd already done the Kurtis Blow and Run-D.M.C. and Jimmy Spicer. LL Cool J could have been one of the first because LL Cool J gave us music. Run-D.M.C. just spit rhymes on top of other people's music. Everybody's still paying their bills with hip-hop. They haven't lost their relationship with their community or with their fans, and their fans are too smart. So you can't really fake for long; you can't have a twenty-five-year career like LL Cool J or Reverend Run unless you're honest.

Funky beats was what I liked a lot, all that James Brown shit, all that funky stuff that was out when I was a kid. And stuff we ended up making the rap records out of. We started a record company because we wanted to manage the process differently. We wanted to make albums, not just singles. We wanted to develop artists that had lasting and stable careers. Not just like disco records—disco mentality managed a lot of the early rap. We saw the Beastie Boys were stars. LL Cool J, Slick Rick, Public Enemy. They weren't just records, you know. And so that's why Def Jam was formed. They were artists and performers. They still are.

We'll tell you what, we won't say *nigger* on mainstream radio. But it doesn't mean that they're not going say it on hip-hop radio. I might not ever use the word referring to a friend, just out of respect for the pain that the community feels, you know. I can see from the outside. I see the sameness that young people see in themselves when they are involved in hip-hop culture—that the Israeli rapper and the Palestinian rapper and the African rapper and the French rapper are all hated by the mainstream, right? It's the only international culture there is. Here's 50 Cent and Eminem, they're the same people. The wants and needs of the people in the trailer park are the same as the wants and needs of the people in the projects. Is 50 Cent really glorifying hard work in the 'hood? Is he saying that his struggle was one that he wishes no one had to go through? Or is he saying let's all go get poor and shoot each other? He's saying the opposite: Pull yourself up.

There's so much cursed action everywhere, you know, and so little consciousness about it. We talk about the three thousand innocent people in the World Trade Center, and everybody gets sad, but never mention the five thousand Africans who died in the last few hours from preventable deaths. We don't talk about the suffering of poor people all over the world.

It's difficult to talk about the gangsta rappers and never mention your gangsta government. We're disconnected. And rappers sometimes connect us, and that's offensive or hurtful or scary. And so we try to escape.

RUSSELL SIMMONS

LORNA SIMPSON

ARTIST

MAHLON DUCKETT

NEGRO LEAGUE BASEBALL PLAYER

1940 ROOKIE OF THE YEAR

WELL, I PLAYED in the forties, and the only difference I could see is that we were just barred from Major League Baseball. But as far as ability in the Negro Leagues, they had as much talent in the Negro Leagues as they did in the Major Leagues. Actually, a lot of people had the wrong idea about Negro Leagues. Most of the games we played were really league games. You know, we had two leagues. Everything in the Negro League was just like

Philadelphia, December 7, 2007

Major League. We had the American League, we had the National League. And we had all-star games every year. And we had the World Series.

After our season was over and the Major League's was over, they used to come up with some ballplayers that would play against us. A lot of the Major League ballplayers wouldn't play against us. This was before Jackie Robinson's time. The one thing that I always thought really changed Major League Baseball was when the Negro League players came in. I mean, they played much harder. You know, we had a lotta ballplayers in the Negro Leagues, they was pretty fast. They'd steal bases. One hit make everyone run. The last great year of the league was, I'd say, '47, because a lot of the ballplayers were back from the service. Another thing about the Negro Leagues, we never had coaches. Our teams had one man that ran the team. That was the manager. And no one was tryin' to help teach you anything because of the fact they were worried about their job. In those days, a lot of the ballplayers in the Major Leagues was only makin' five or six dollars an hour. We would play, say, eighteen-, twenty-game series in different towns. That's what they called the barnstorming tour. Now, every year they had two great teams. They had the Bob Feller All-Stars, for which he tried to get the cream from the Major Leagues, and Satchel Paige. And Satchel tried to get the cream from the Negro Leagues. In 1940 I was voted the Rookie of the Year from the league. And I was one of the ballplayers that was picked to play in this all-star game. So I was a little shaky 'cause our first game was in Washington, D.C., at Griffith Stadium. But the first time I came to bat, I hit a double to right-center field. I'll never forget it. The next time I came up, I hit one to left field. And I was slidin' into second base, because in those days, I was pretty fast. Second time, I got up on second base. I said to myself, "It doesn't matter the color of the skin." And that's what changed my mind. And that was true. It was true because we had so many great pitchers in our league. But we didn't get the recognition in 1940. And I, you know, I was still a little leery. You know, all your Joe DiMaggios, and all that kind of stuff.

Well, I played with the Homestead Grays for two years when the league was getting ready to break up. I wasn't there when Josh Gibson was, although I played hundreds of games against Josh. We all thought Josh was the greatest hitter in baseball, and people still say the same thing.

THE ONE THING THAT I ALWAYS THOUGHT REALLY CHANGED MAJOR LEAGUE BASEBALL WAS WHEN THE NEGRO LEAGUE PLAYERS CAME IN. I MEAN, THEY PLAYED MUCH HARDER.

He was a personal friend of mine. When I came up, I was only a kid outta high school. Josh was big, about six-foot-three. A lot of people just knew Josh by his hitting. But Josh was a great catcher. He could throw. Plus he could run for his size. I think the New York *Amsterdam News* really kept up with the Negro Leagues. But below Washington, a lot of towns didn't even have press at the game. So that's why our stats was never accurate. You know, they never could tell you exactly what you was hitting, your battin' average and so forth. And so, it was just a shame. So a lot of people askin' me about Josh say, "Well, we heard that Josh hit at least nine hundred home runs." And I would tell the audience or whoever asked me, "Well, look, I can't tell you exactly how many because I thought he hit nine hundred against *us*."

You see, like I said, I played in the forties. And that's when they had all that segregation down there. And they had the Ku Klux Klan. We played in towns, especially, like, in Alabama, and Mississippi, and so forth, where they had curfews on black people. To me it was a disgrace. Even when the fans came out, they had a curfew of ten o'clock. If the game was still going on, they would have to leave, be off the streets. And to me, it was heartbreaking, you know, 'cause I never was used to anything like that. After we went below Washington, a lot of people heard about the Negro League. And, you know, they called us all kinda names. But a lot of white people, they said, "Boy, I've never seen a ball game like that," you know.

When we went out on the field, we played for the love of the game. We couldn't say we played for the money, 'cause the money wasn't there. But we played to win. You get a base hit, next time you came to bat, the ball would be at your head, you know. All of 'em did it but Satchel. Satchel would never throw at you—I don't know why. I had pretty good success against Satchel. I would never fear Satchel, you know, as far as throwin' at your head. If you remember, we didn't have helmets in those days. I was hit in the head twice. But that was just part of the game. We got Leon Day; he was my buddy, too. I was the pallbearer at his funeral. And, you know, he'd throw at me. I said,

"Leon, hey. You know, I thought we was all right." He said, "We are. But now you hittin', like, .280. Well, gotta keep you from hitting .281."

I've often thought about if I had gone in and went through a farm system, you know, where they had people tellin' me what I was doin' wrong, and so forth and so on. It coulda been different. But who knows? I came down with rheumatic fever. Don't know how I caught it, 'cause rheumatic fever's usually a child disease. But I was going on thirty years old. A lot of those great ballplayers was really too old for the Major Leagues to be signin' anyway. When the league broke up, they lost their jobs. And that's the only thing I can say against Jackie. But I was so glad because it opened the door for everyone. As far as attendance, 1949 was terrible. And that's because everyone, they were just waiting for Jackie, you know.

I never even knew who the scouts were. We heard they were out there. But I never personally met a scout. But they said they was at the ballparks lookin', so forth and so on. And I guess they was because Jackie went up to the majors in '47. And they didn't take too many ballplayers until the fifties. Willie Mays didn't come up till '51. But in the late forties, it was only a few that were signed and they really didn't get the swing of things until, I would say, the fifties. Ernie Banks, all of 'em came up '52, '53, and so forth. But it's Ed Sullivan that had the *Toast of the Town*, that program. He was one of the fellows that came out and said, "Well, we got blacks gettin' killed in the war," and so forth. I

don't know what happened between Ed Sullivan and Major League Baseball. But it had that commissioner, Kenesaw Mountain Landis, sayin' the black man will never play as long as he was commissioner. But we thought it would happen before Jackie. Against us, Jackie never played that much. He'd pitch it in. A couple times he played third base. I could tell he was very fast. And the ball he hit, he hit pretty hard. But he wasn't a regular in the Kansas City Monarchs infield. So my thoughts was because of Jackie's background. I said, "Maybe Branch Rickey is takin' Jackie because the people was all about black ballplayers going to the Major Leagues." I said, "Now we give Jackie a chance, and he don't make it, say, well we did it," you know. Well, Jackie went up there. He turned out to be one of the best ballplayers in our time. But I had thought at the time, everyone was talking about Larry Doby. And that's who we had heard that the black ballplayer was going to be. A lot of people thought that some of the ballplayers resented Jackie. Well, we didn't. All the ballplayers I talked to, they was like me. They were so glad to have heard that Jackie was gonna get that trial because of the fact I said, "Well, it will open the door even if Jackie don't make it, so we're much sooner down the line than, you know, if he didn't." But, you know, he turned out to be so great.

WHEN WE WENT OUT ON THE FIELD, WE PLAYED FOR THE LOVE OF THE GAME. WE COULDN'T SAY WE PLAYED FOR THE MONEY, 'CAUSE THE MONEY WASN'T THERE.

MAHLON DUCKETT

ZANE

EROTIC AUTHOR
PUBLISHER

I WANTED TO tackle many things with the book *Addicted*—that women are very sexual beings and do have needs just like men. I made the central character in that book and the book that followed it a black female psychiatrist, because of the fact that I know it's often considered a stigma of weakness to seek psychiatric help in the African-American community.

New York City, September 21, 2007

I started out as self-published. Now I'm publishing five books a month by other people in addition to my own books. I was very hidden. In fact, my parents didn't even know I had a book out until I had three on the *Essence* best-seller list at the same time. So then I said, "OK. I think it's about time I tell them." No one knew that I was Zane, including my own family. My mother, I told her in the car one day: "Remember when I talked about writing a book under another name and putting it out?" And she said, "Oh, you really did it, didn't you?" So I had her stop by the drugstore. I went in and got an issue of *Essence,* and I showed her these three books on the best-seller list. And I said, "That's me." And it was really cute, because now my mother walks around with *Sex Chronicles* T-shirts on and all that stuff.

> MY PARENTS DIDN'T EVEN KNOW I HAD A BOOK OUT UNTIL I HAD THREE ON THE *ESSENCE* BEST-SELLER LIST AT THE SAME TIME.

My father is actually a theologian. When my mother said, "Your father read *Nervous,*" the only thing that flashed in my mind was all of the sex scenes. But he thought it was a brilliant book because it deals with a woman with multiple personality disorder that was brought about because she was a victim of incest as a child. My mother did at one point say, "Can you write a book that the people at the church can read?" And I said, "Well, believe it or not, they probably already read my books." A lot of people read my books and think they are fiction, but I get mail all the time from women who are going through stuff much, much deeper than the things in my book.

I started out over the internet writing short stories. I never actually wanted to be a book author. I wrote one short story in November of 1997, and I sent it out to four or five friends. I ended up putting *First Night, The Airport*, and *The Seduction* on my AOL web space. And after three weeks, I emailed back to forty, fifty people who had emailed me. And within three weeks, my AOL site got eight thousand hits by word of mouth alone before it was taken down because of the content. At that point, I knew that I could sell a book. I got approached by a lot of publishers who wanted to publish me. But they said that I was too wild, and they wanted me to write a typically black romance novel or a sister-girl kind of novel. I refused. I ended up putting *The Sex Chronicles* out in May of 2000. And immediately all the distributors are like, "Wow, there really is a *Sex Chronicles*?" 'Cause they had gotten so many phone calls about it. That immediately sold over one hundred thousand copies. And the rest just kinda goes from there.

92

I always tell people, I am a huge Prince fan. In all honesty, I liked his boldness. I like the fact that he's a risk taker. And I felt, like, in many ways with publishing, I'm the same way.

I actually have met someone masquerading as me in Jamaica, of all places. There was a lady over there pretending to be me. I sat there and let her talk. And eventually I told her that I really was Zane. She was really embarrassed. It turned out she was a bookstore manager from Florida.

My mother had me take speed-reading when I was in third grade. And by the sixth grade, I was reading a book a day. *My Daddy Was a Numbers Runner,* when I first read it, the scene in the movie theater just blew my mind. I grew up in a house full of books. We actually had a second basement that probably had somewhere between eight thousand and ten thousand books in it. As a child, when I was given creative writing assignments, I would always turn in the weirdest, wildest stories. When I was younger, all of my teachers always told me I was gonna be a writer when I grew up. I never believed them, 'cause it does come very, very easy to me, writing. I knew that it would sell. But I never knew it would become as widespread and everything as it did. On tour for *Dear G-Spot,* I went to a bookstore, and they had a big  stand out front with *Dear G-Spot* at the top and the Harry Potter book at the bottom. I took a picture of that, 'cause I thought that was funny.

To be honest with you, if I was not publishing other people, I probably would have remained anonymous forever. But I knew I needed to go out and help promote them and support them. Because they had put their faith in me as their publisher, that's really the main reason why I decided to so-called come out. I had a bunch of famous writers who were on my e-mail list who read my stories. And all of them said, "You're gonna kill your career if you actually put out a book like that. Write something else." They told me the same thing. And it's ironic, because now a lot of them are like, "Zane, my next book is an erotic book. It's an erotic thriller." Or "I'm gonna be in this erotica anthology."

ZANE

Now it's become the hip thing. And so it's funny to me every time I hear from a writer who told me not to do it, that now they're going to write erotica. All of them wanted me to change what I was doing. They didn't think that it would sell. I knew that the market existed for it. And it's the same way, again, with things that I publish. I publish a lot of books that other publishers would not touch. I have an open mind, and I realize that even if I'm not going through that particular situation, even if I've never dealt with the particular subject, I know that there's a market out there for people dealing with all types of things. I was shocked the first time I walked into a bookstore and saw *The Sex Chronicles* right in the front of the store, five shelves of it. I never thought that would happen. I thought it was going to end up being an underground kind

of thing. I knew that it would sell, but I never knew it would become as widespread as it did. I feel a huge responsibility now when I am writing. There's certain things that I would not put out there simply because I don't want to start a trend.

I am very conscious of the fact that a lot of women look to me for advice and what they should really do in their own lives. I feel that if women are gonna have sex during their lifetime, and the majority of women are, there's no reason that they should walk away from the experience any less satisfied than the man. My whole thing is that I hope that by reading my books and getting caught up in the characters, women will realize that they're entitled to make demands. But I do get some very, very serious, serious emails. I was at a book signing, and a lady actually came up to me and fell into my arms crying, and told me that she realized that if she didn't get help for what happened to her as a child, that she was gonna turn into the main character of my book; she did not want to end up like that. If I had written a manual on sexual addiction, nobody would have really read it. But by doing it as a fiction-based story, where people get caught up in the character and that kind of stuff, it can have almost the same impact as an actual manual would.

With *Afterburn*, I had just lost a very close friend of mine who was told that he wouldn't live past the age of five. He had three brain surgeries by the age of five. Had sickle-cell anemia. And he actually lived until he was twenty-nine. But the thing about him—his name was Kevin Shiffley— is that he was the happiest person I'd ever met. Even though he was in and out of hospitals his entire life, you know, always in the hospital, he was happy. He never complained, whereas other people could break a nail or get a flat tire, and it's almost like the end of the world. So, at that point, that's the reason I decided to take that direction with that book, because I saw so many people wasting valuable time on really stupid things.

I FEEL THAT IF WOMEN ARE GONNA HAVE SEX DURING THEIR LIFETIME, AND THE MAJORITY OF WOMEN ARE, THERE'S NO REASON THAT THEY SHOULD WALK AWAY FROM THE EXPERIENCE ANY LESS SATISFIED THAN THE MAN.

ZANE

AL SHARPTON

REVEREND

CIVIL RIGHTS ACTIVIST

2004 PRESIDENTIAL CANDIDATE

THIRTY-SEVENTH PSALM: There are two parts to that psalm that I always think of. "Fret not thyself because of evildoers." And then I like to go down to the twenty-third verse, which talks about "the steps of a good man is ordered by the Lord." And around the twenty-fifth verse, it says, "I have been young. Now I'm old. But I've never seen the righteous forsaken." But the strange thing—I've never said this publicly—is James Brown used

New York City, October 2, 2007

to read that psalm all the time. When he went to jail, when he would be facing some kind of difficulty. And when he died, I was with his children when they opened up his house to claim his personal effects. And next to his bed was the Bible opened to the thirty-seventh psalm.

I'll never forget the first time I met him to talk to him was backstage at New York Symphony Space. He said he wanted to do a memorial show for his son, and he would give the money to my youth group: "You do it my way. You listen. I'll tell you how to promote this. Your youth group, I'll put it on the map. I'll put it on the map. But you can't go for nothin' small with me. Go for the whole hog." And I'm trying to understand what all this means. And we're walking with him. He's walking out of the dressing room now, and talking. And the next thing I know, he grabs the mike and starts singing. We had actually walked on stage with him. And in the middle of this conversation, he goes into his opening set. So I'm standing there, and thousands of people are out there screaming. I don't know what to do. So I start dancing, like I was supposed to do it, and got myself off the stage. Two weeks later, he had me going to California and introduced me on *Soul Train*. And started a thirty-five-year bond that ended when he died.

He was very short. About 5'5", 5'6". Very compact. Very much in shape. But he had this overbearing presence. I traveled with him a lot, went all over the world with him. And you could bring a guy seven foot tall in the room with James Brown, and he still seemed taller than the other guy. It was just this dominating kind of presence he had that's hard to describe to people that were never around him. Even in private, he just had this kind of personality. And even his normal everyday movement, he was just different. He was a different kind of person. And I think about how he never doubted his place in history. It gives me a lot of solace to think about that when I'm facing a controversy, which, compared to stuff he went through, was nothing. And he ended up being right.

There were maybe two or three blacks before him that went mainstream. Nat King Cole, people like that. But James Brown was the first one that made mainstream go black. He became like the father I didn't have because my parents separated when I was ten. I learned a lot of civil rights and politics being around Shirley Chisholm and Jesse Jackson and others.

> I LEARNED A LOT OF CIVIL RIGHTS AND POLITICS BEING AROUND SHIRLEY CHISHOLM AND JESSE JACKSON AND OTHERS. BUT I LEARNED MANHOOD FROM JAMES BROWN.

But I learned manhood from James Brown. I guess even subconsciously, when I would come back to New York and begin activism, and we were still close, I brought that into my activism of not backing up or not caring if it became controversial. Believing in the picture you painted in your own mind, I got that from James Brown. In fact, he loved controversy. He would say, "That's good. You want everybody talkin' about it because that's the point, to move forward."

I felt I became the preacher side of him 'cause he molded and shaped me in the image I think he would have been as a preacher. I guess growing up in entertainment became part of my orientation. And the good of that is that the theatrics sometimes helps attract a lot of people. The bad of that is that you get the nay-sayers who think it's too theatrical. In many ways, the civil rights move-ment is theatrics. Martin Luther King used theatrics, Birmingham, the drama of marching, the drama of kids going to jail. Part of that, of course, is deep, hard struggle. But the theatrics of it in a media age brings the point home. Absent that, you're sitting in some university trying to explain what drama drives home.

The reason why the black church and the black minister became so dominant in the struggle is we didn't have black politicians or black profes-sionals. They were the only ones that were independent enough and had a platform to speak from. And even now, they're still freer than politicians. It was one of the few places we could assemble. It was one of the few places where whites did not dictate the program. You gotta remember, most blacks, if you were a boy or a girl or a maid or whatever during the week, you were chairman of deacon board on Sunday. This was the first place you had a title. So the church was not only our spiritual home, it was our social and our political and our economic headquarters. Black colleges started there. Black businesses started there. It was our lives. You judge a tree's strength by how deep its roots run underground. And the black church was the roots for us.

I wanted to run for president because I wanted to put us in the debate. I wanted to bring the fact that even in the twenty-first century, we've still not dealt with the question of race. We've still not solved the questions of the imbalance in the criminal justice system. And I calculated that going in. I knew it was unlikely I'd be president even if everybody running against me died; they would have found a way to go and make somebody else president. But I knew that once I got on that stage, they couldn't control the debate.

I had a black conservative tell me on a talk show once, "You gotta remember, I didn't make it because of civil rights. Civil rights didn't write my résumé." I said, "Yeah, but civil rights made somebody *read* your résumé. You weren't the first qualified Negro in America." No matter how eloquently somebody says we're beyond race, we're not. Just look at the facts. We are still doubly unemployed to whites in America today. We still are incarcerated at a higher rate for the same criminal accusations, same criminal background. We still are three times more likely to be turned down for a bank loan with the same credit, same income.

And I think that's what you're seeing in the hip-hop generation: this disconnect, this dislocation. We're not grounding these kids anymore. I was one of those kids. If James Brown hadn't happened to me, I would have probably been a gang member or a drug seller. We told them you're free now. It's beyond race. You don't need all of that. And we gave them nothing to replace it. And then we look up in ten years and say, What's wrong with these kids? What's wrong with them is, there's nothing grounding them. You're connected to nothing. And you have these distorted visions imposed upon you of what manhood is. So manhood becomes thugism or hoodlumism. Or not, Did you go to college, but, Did you do your time in jail? Or you're a real man 'cause you got shot.

You actually have some black kids being told that to be smart and eloquent is to act white. Well, who decided after two centuries of struggling for educational excellence that being a thug now is the definition of black manhood? Our community was always trying to break down barriers and do better. But this imposed culture is almost like a twenty-first-century version of racism that you act the fool. It's a new way of step and fetch it. And they've become the gangsterized thug Uncle Toms that entertain whites' worst opinion of black folks. Anytime you study our history, we used our art to reach up, whether it was Paul Robeson or Marian Anderson. It wasn't just to reflect what you see. It was to look at what wasn't there and put everybody's mind toward trying to be that. In slavery we sang, "Go Down, Moses," "Swing Low, Sweet Chariot." We weren't singing about niggers in the field picking cotton. Our art never just reflected what was there. It also was a vision of what wasn't there, and it helped move a people toward that. And that's what I think we've lost. And that's what we've gotta get back.

NO MATTER HOW ELOQUENTLY SOMEBODY SAYS WE'RE BEYOND RACE, WE'RE NOT. JUST LOOK AT THE FACTS.

AL SHARPTON

KAREEM
ABDUL-JABBAR

BASKETBALL PLAYER

  (MILWAUKEE BUCKS, 1969–1974;

  LOS ANGELES LAKERS, 1975–1989)

AUTHOR

I HAVE A HOUSE now on 120th Street, but I don't have much time to spend there because I'm out here coaching for the Lakers. So I haven't been spending a lot of time there. But talk about people who had the gift of foresight. James Weldon Johnson, in 1927, said, "At some point, the real estate in Harlem is gonna become so valuable, and it's too bad that most of the people who now live here don't understand the value of owning the

Los Angeles, September 12, 2007

homes that they live in." And it took eighty years. I grew up in Inwood, the northern end of Manhattan. It was a Revolutionary War battlefield. There's also a house on Broadway about 204th Street that was an old Dutch farmhouse, from the time that New York was New Amsterdam. So I always had a sense of being someplace where things had happened earlier. We used to find musket balls and arrowheads and really old bottles in vacant lots and places in that neighborhood that had been there since Colonial times. So I

was always fascinated with what had gone before me. But I think a lot more of it had to do with my grandmother. My family's from the West Indies, and the whole idea of telling stories and keeping family history alive certainly was a part of it.

Things were very difficult for my father. If he'd had his dream, he would've played in Count Basie's band; that would've made him the happiest person in the world. He would've done that until the day he died.

And he never got that opportunity. So he became a police officer and did very well as a police officer. He retired. He was a lieutenant. But, you know, music really was his heart, his love. He played in Benny Carter's band for a while there. And he got an offer to tour with Ray Charles in 1960, but he wasn't able to take advantage of it.

It was my freshman year at UCLA, and they had a jazz festival down in Orange County at the fairgrounds. And Miles Davis's band played. I knew Tony Williams, Wayne Shorter, and Ron Carter very well. So I went down to check him out and they introduced me. And he looks at me and says, "It must cost you about five hundred dollars to get a necktie." And then he just kept goin'. And it's like, wow! That's not the type of thing that you expect that's gonna happen when you meet your hero. You expect a more meaningful moment. But within the next two years, playing for UCLA and doing as well as we did, I came to Miles's attention.

Then I ran into him on 135th Street. He'd been working out at the Y there. And he knew who I was at that point. It was like we were all friends. He invited me to his home. We watched some fight film, just hung out for the rest of the day. It was just nice to be around Miles, to see how he was always aware that there were eyes out there; you know, like the walls have eyes. And Miles always maintained a certain public decorum because of that. He was always impeccably dressed. I would go into the gym with Wilt Chamberlain, and Miles would usually be there. I mean, I must've seen him in there eight, ten times on different occasions when I'd go in there with Wilt. He did a serious boxing workout: heavy bag, jump rope, shadow box, speed bag. And you could tell he was in great condition.

Louis Armstrong was able to do both things at the same time—be himself and still be an advocate for civil rights. That's a very difficult thing for people to do. Because they get overcome with anger and the need to say those things. But he kept a great sense of balance. Talking with Ossie Davis about Louis, he said that he could be that way because he had a dagger in his trumpet. He could get the pain and the anger out through his art. And, you know, that relieved him of having to carry it with him all the time.

> I THINK TOO MANY PEOPLE IN THE NBA ARE JUST VERY COMFORTABLE GETTING THE WONDERFUL OPPORTUNITIES THAT THEY HAVE TO BE WEALTHY AND ENJOY WHAT THEY DO AND HAVE A PROFESSIONAL LIFE. AND THEY DON'T REALLY UNDERSTAND HOW IT GOT TO THAT POINT.

I'm just happy to see that people with talent, like Tony Dungy and Lovie Smith, are being given opportunities, no matter where they are. That's becoming more and more of a trend now. And people are sometimes shocked to see that someone who's doing something is Black or Hispanic or a woman. But nowadays that's more and more the case. Talented people are getting the opportunities that they deserve. I'm glad that John Carlos and Tommie Williams went and did what they did at the 1968 Olympics. Because somebody needed to make a statement there. I didn't go. I stayed home and worked. I needed to make money so I could get out of college. I wanted to graduate. So I was glad that they did what they did. Somebody needed to say something about the way that the Olympics were being used for political means.

I was at the game, November 1960, when Elgin Baylor scored seventy-one points against the Knicks. I was thirteen years old. And then, coaching for the Lakers, I saw Kobe get his eighty-one points. It's amazing. My first game in the NBA was against the Pistons at Milwaukee, and they had Walt Bellamy. I passed him about three times at one point, going from offense to defense, and he never got out of the midcourt area. And he said, "Slow down. You're gonna make me look bad." That was something that really made me appreci-

KAREEM ABDUL-JABBAR

ate playing for John Wooden, the fact that I didn't have to be a bruiser. I wasn't gonna be Wilt. I didn't have that type of bulk and, you know, physical presence. But I did have speed and agility, and I could make an impact on the game using my talents.

Basketball is a very telegenic game. It fits on the screen just right. You can see things in a close-up that you can't see on a football field or a baseball diamond. So basketball had the potential to be viewed in ways that the other popular sports didn't. The Milwaukee Bucks tried to send me

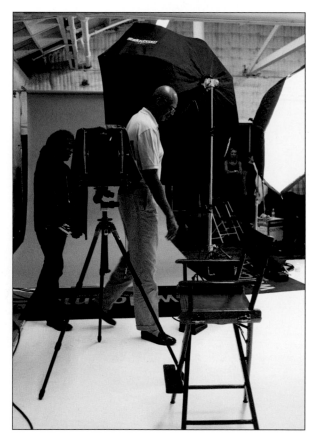

to the Knicks, but the Knicks didn't have many players. All they had was money. And the Lakers had players and money. It was an easy deal, and coming back to L.A. was OK with me. I wanted to play for the Knicks, but it just wasn't in the cards.

You had great athletes playing the game with the abandon and the ability to do certain things. You had myself. You had Dr. J.; he thrilled a few people with his stuff. And you had George Gervin and Earl Monroe. I mean, certain guys, if you see them play, it strikes you, and you wanna see more. There were some guys that came in the league that were just incredible athletes; just watching them was an extraordinary pleasure. I think a whole lot of things just clicked at one time. The opportunity and the available talent were superior. And everybody had their own statement to make on the court. I think too many people in the NBA are just very comfortable getting the wonderful opportunities that they have to be wealthy and enjoy what they do and have a professional life. And they don't really understand how it got to that point. If they knew what the Harlem Wrens went through, pushing a bus in the middle of winter and stuff like that, they would have a different attitude about it. But a lot of these facts get lost in the mists of time.

President Kennedy left out a few people when he wrote his book *Profiles in Courage*. So I wanted to get it across that there was more to that story than what everybody assumed. I started writing when I was in grade school. And at one point, I wanted to be a journalism major. I thought about going to Columbia and the University of Missouri; they both have journalism schools. But basketball kind of loomed there. So I went to UCLA and was an English major. The quote I have in the book that I usually go back to is: "I'd rather be a lamppost in Harlem than governor of Georgia." People don't understand a black American saying that, but it's so true. Being someplace that you are accepted and encouraged to be at your best, having a community like that—where in the rest of America you face hostility and oppression—it means a lot. I remember a friend of mine had been away from home for two years, playing basketball. When he got back to New York, he took the train right up to 125th Street and just walked the length of 125th Street and started crying. Because he was so happy to be back in that cradle.

KAREEM ABDUL-JABBAR

WILLIAM RICE

TUSKEGEE AIRMAN

THE TUSKEGEE AIRMEN were the first to break ground for the Negro pilots. And come December '44, we got our orders to go overseas. So they gave us time off to go home, visit the folks and everything. They put us on one of those little old Liberty ships, loaded down with locomotives, and trucks, and everything else. They shipped us to Italy. That's where the 332nd was located, a little strip on the Adriatic Sea. And there they acquainted us

Philadelphia, December 7, 2007

with the P-51 Mustang, which was a beautiful airplane. I spent my time with the 100th Fighter Squad. Captain Andrew Turner, he was my squadron CO. And all during the war, that's where I flew thirty-four missions.

I grew up—well, it wasn't on a farm, but it was out in the sticks. And I used to see National Guard airplanes flying over and also dirigibles that the navy had. I've always been interested in flying. I was in the United States Army Air Corps, something I'd always wanted to do when I was a kid. I lived in the North, and I went to a Northern high school. And we weren't segregated.

So, segregation, it was never on my mind at the time. But I knew about it. In November of 1942, I was in high school. I came into Philadelphia to enlist. And they inducted me. I left Philadelphia and went to Fort Meade, Maryland, where I stayed for about two weeks. I left Washington, D.C., at night, on a Pullman. So the next morning, when I got down in Nashville, they yanked me and put me up front with the rest of the colored people. And that's where I stayed till I got to Biloxi. And that's where I really ran into segregation, Jim Crow, and all that. Then the orders came through, to send me on to Tuskegee. I was glad to get out of Mississippi, believe me.

Some of the Southerners thought we were monkeys or something. The only segregation overseas was from the people in the air force from the South. In Rome, during V-J Day, we were partying. I was a first lieutenant. And we had a Southern ground officer making slurs about black people. So we ignored him. But, actually, most of the bomber groups never knew we were black. We escorted them day in and day out, but they had no idea that we were a Negro fighter group escorting them. None of my instructors were black, except the ones in primary training, which were on the campus. But after primary, all the instructors were white. I had a white instructor from Boston. He told me that they wash out better pilots than graduated with him. That's because they had a quota. They couldn't graduate but so many men at a time. Toward the war's end, I don't think they could get enough pilots to graduate. We had a large class when I came through in '44. But after that, the classes started to dwindle. I was in Tuskegee in '46, when the last class graduated. I think they only had about ten or twelve men at that time graduating.

During the Korean War, around 1949, I got a letter from the air force, asking me if I wanted to return to service. I politely turned it down. I said no way. I went to work for the Pennsylvania Railroad. And I spent more time being furloughed, because every time they had a strike, I was furloughed. I stuck with them for about a year or two, off and on. Then I came out to Meade here, in Delaware County. And I got a job at a block plant. They made cinder and cement blocks. I worked off and on there for about five years. But in 1952, I went to work for Piasecki. They built helicopters. And I stayed with them for forty-one years. The name changed from Piasecki to Vertol; from Vertol to Boeing Helicopters. And that's where I retired.

MOST OF THE BOMBER GROUPS NEVER KNEW WE WERE BLACK. WE ESCORTED THEM DAY IN AND DAY OUT, BUT THEY HAD NO IDEA THAT WE WERE A NEGRO FIGHTER GROUP ESCORTING THEM.

I had joined the Philadelphia chapter of the Tuskegee Airmen briefly. They were meeting at night. And that's when I worked at night, so I didn't stay there too long. I had to drop out of that, because I couldn't be missing time to attend the meetings. But I kept in contact with them. And I know most of the men that belonged to that chapter.

WILLIAM RICE

THELMA GOLDEN

DIRECTOR AND CHIEF CURATOR,
THE STUDIO MUSEUM IN HARLEM

FOR ME, I THINK that being able to present the work of black artists is really my passion. So the idea of being a curator invested in black art, presenting their work, presenting the ways in which they work, and really being part of an institution that's devoted to that is incredibly important to me. The Whitney Museum was an interesting situation for me because, on one hand, as someone who's just interested in art—all kinds of art, art from

New York City, November 21, 2006

all areas—it was amazing to work at this New York institution that really defined American art and in many ways had defined the way in which contemporary art had been shown. But I could not be at the Whitney and not acknowledge the legacy of exclusion in some ways. And so I felt that while I was there, I had to find ways to think about how to intervene into the Whitney's history, to look back at its past, and understand and embrace those moments in the Whitney's past when black artists were not at the forefront, but also to point out those moments when the institution had taken a stand and included black artists in the collection or in exhibitions.

I became a curator at a moment where there hadn't been many black curators in mainstream institutions in this country. In many ways, when we're talking about correctives, when we're talking about the way images can hurt, there is also a way that for some people images can heal. So having images, representational images, that reflect what people know about themselves, or what they want to be in themselves, or what they want their children to see, representation is the way in which one gets at that. So there's a way in which oil painters who work in a representational style, making images of black people, will always have a place in black culture.

In my own home, I grew up with a range of art. You know, one of the most interesting art experiences I had as a child is that I grew up around this series of sculptures of black heroes that were created and commissioned by some alcohol company. It was something that you could buy. If you bought this alcohol, you could buy it from the back of the box. They were created by an artist named Inge Hardison, a black woman sculptor—not known enough, certainly, but someone who was doing incredible work looking at various different art traditions at that time. And I realize on one level how this was sort of one of these gift-with-purchase sort of situations, the art that you got. I think that I was influenced by things that weren't necessarily shown in museums or came out of galleries.

I don't think it's a responsibility of black artists to feel that they have to be engaged in politics or in the culture. I actually believe that it is the freedom that artists might choose for themselves that is the radical gesture. We also have a tradition of artists who have made work for the pure pleasure and joy and beauty that art can bring. So while, yes, I feel that in my

...WHEN WE'RE TALKING ABOUT CORRECTIVES, WHEN WE'RE TALKING ABOUT THE WAY IMAGES CAN HURT, THERE IS ALSO A WAY THAT FOR SOME PEOPLE IMAGES CAN HEAL.

work I have responsibility to black artists, to black culture—to present it, to examine it, to be involved in it in ways that move it forward—I also feel that I have a responsibility to do that with a certain kind of passion and a certain kind of pleasure as well.

Probably the first artist that excited me after getting to know his work as a child would have been Jean-Michel Basquiat. I was a high school student in New York City at the time that the East Village and SoHo scene began. At that time, Jean-Michel was working, and his work was very prescient. He had a role and a place in the New York art world at that moment that made him extraordinarily unique. And it was through my understanding or even my discovery of his work—'cause I can't say at that point I understood his work—that it really opened for me the sense of what the art world was, how museums could work, and what museums were about.

I'm not sure what "selling out" means. I think some people term it to mean that there can't be validity in one's work as a black artist if somehow that artist benefits from it financially or even in terms of fame. Because as the art-and-culture world remains somewhat exclusive, this idea of barriers being broken sometimes can be positioned as selling out.

That is, if there are spaces that we have not entered, and an artist enters them, often there's a question about why they're there. I don't see it that way at all. I sort of see the possibility as that all the spaces we haven't entered, we should be entering. And you know that for many black people, early in this century, even to the middle of this century, being an artist was not an option. So what's so amazing about the black community, you find a kind of artistry in all forms. What we call an artist in the black community also has to be widened often because, truly, sometimes it does not exist within an art context.

I think that my goal is to add to the conversation by presenting artists. Because I think that artists have so much to say about who we are and where we live and what our culture is and is becoming. And so by being able to make exhibitions that put artists out there in the forefront, it allows the public an entry into that dialogue. Because images are so powerful and there are many ways in which, in the African-American community, people

THELMA GOLDEN

see art having a role. People want to live around images that in many ways negate the images that are out there in popular culture, or even sometimes in the mainstream press. They want to see images of the people who they think are important. They want to see images that they think reflect the beauty of African-American culture. And often that can take an incredibly romantic, even sentimental point of view. I made an exhibition about this a couple years ago called "Black Romantic," looking at the ways in which black people sometimes can desire art to do and be certain things as it relates to our own relationship, to how powerful and hurtful images in the world can be. Those artists ranged from those who were simply taking on the subject of black culture, making the kinds of pictures that they felt came out of their own experience and their own history, to artists who had more of a political agenda, who were creating images of black heroes, of black figures in a way that commemorated and memorialized them and created for people the opportunity to live with those images in their homes.

> I DON'T THINK IT'S A RESPONSIBILITY OF BLACK ARTISTS TO FEEL THAT THEY HAVE TO BE ENGAGED IN POLITICS OR IN THE CULTURE. I ACTUALLY BELIEVE THAT IT IS THE FREEDOM THAT ARTISTS MIGHT CHOOSE FOR THEMSELVES THAT IS THE RADICAL GESTURE.

Every day people call the museum advocating for an artist either in their family or in their community, often an artist who worked in a way that has not been known. Sometimes this is long after their death and the work is discovered. Quite often what it brings up is the way in which many artists in our community often work anonymously.

I had the amazing opportunity of working at the Metropolitan Museum as an intern when I was in high school. And just walking through those galleries and seeing the art of so many cultures was an amazing experience for me. It's really how I decided I wanted to spend my life in a museum. And the only way to be able to do that was to work in one, really. One of the funniest experiences I had when I began working in the art world was that people always assumed I worked *for* Thelma Golden, not that I *was* Thelma Golden. I mean, certainly racism has existed in the art world as it has in the rest of the world.

You know, we live now in a moment where there are examples of black artists making their work in the world and doing it successfully. And I think that's what this generation, my generation, owes the generations before us, the fact that there are real examples. And those examples are embedded and written into the history of recent art history in ways that make it not impossible to think of being an artist within the black community. Because at this moment, for the first time, the work that so many people have done through this century to document the contributions of black artists is visible. There are artists whose legacies are well known, they stand within the canon of American art at this point. This moment is the great beneficiary of all of that work. There was a way in which exclusion was the norm in museums. And there certainly was an attitude that the work was not good enough or the artist could not possibly be important or good because they were black. But that's also what created the opportunity to have museums like the Studio Museum. It's what created the museums and the collections at many of the historically black colleges and universities. Within the community, of course, it was known that there was power and beauty and quality in this work. And the black community didn't always wait for the mainstream to sanction it.

THELMA GOLDEN

SEAN COMBS

MOGUL

ACTOR

FOUNDER, BAD BOY RECORDS

THERE WERE A LOT of people saying that I was crazy for trying to pursue a profession that you couldn't get an education for in a college. I would walk around with my briefcase and say that I was going to be the next Berry Gordy, and I was gonna be a music manager, and I was gonna be a mogul one day.

New York City, January 9, 2008

The first artist I signed on my own was the Notorious B.I.G. I first met Biggie in early 1993 at Sylvia's Restaurant in Harlem. I was looking for someone to kind of rival LL Cool J, a sex-symbol type. I had called around, and I had asked if anybody knew of any new talent. And when I met him, it wasn't really what I was looking for at the time, because I was looking for, you know, a nice caramel complexion. I was really looking for a cliché: curly haired, light-skinned cat, you know. Bobby Brown, he was breaking through, but light skin was still really in. Biggie was blacker than ever. To be honest, I haven't signed any light-skinned guys. I've stuck with the chocolate all my life.

Biggie was raw, you know, he was the truth. Sometimes it was almost like he was a thesis to getting into the inner workings of the young black mind during the late eighties, early nineties. The struggles that we were going through, and how we felt. The thing that really shocked people was when Biggie admitted that being young and black and living in America makes you feel like you want to kill yourself.

THE THING THAT REALLY SHOCKED PEOPLE WAS WHEN BIGGIE ADMITTED THAT BEING YOUNG AND BLACK AND LIVING IN AMERICA MAKES YOU FEEL LIKE YOU WANT TO KILL YOURSELF.

I just wanted to be somebody; my whole life has been not facing reality, you know, living and acquiring the dream. If you were coming up in the late eighties, during the time of crack, you were either gonna be on crack or be in jail, or just die. The dreams that I was having when I was walking around telling people, people actually thought that I was crazy. I think you had to be a little crazy to really make it out of that time.

I think the moment that I really realized that I had started to become who I wanted to become was when I was walking down Times Square, and they had just put up a new billboard of myself. I was getting a lot of pushback, because I wanted to put up a billboard in Times Square with a fist in the air. And this is the home of that redneck white Marlboro Man. Now you got this young black guy, and he has the biggest billboard in Times Square. It's, like, fifty stories high, and they know the whole world's gonna come to New York and see this message of black power, with my fist in the air. I didn't realize it was gonna be that big, so when they had put it up, I went and walked in Times Square, and I just stood and looked up at myself for, like, three hours. And it wasn't an ego thing. It was like, "Now maybe people are finally going to get what I'm about." The motivation was never money. It was about always inspiring my people that we could do it, that it doesn't just have to be a dream. That it can be a reality.

If you study black history, it's just so negative, you know. It's just like, OK, we were slaves, and then we were whipped and sprayed with water hoses, and the civil rights movement, and we're American gangsters. I get motivated for us to be seen in our brilliance. And that's the way I always wanted it to be in my fashion. A lot of people from the hip-hop community sometimes think that it's materialism. But when you're coming up in the crack era, in the eighties, and you get a chance to get it, and you get a chance to live better, I'd rather show kids that than to constantly see the cutaways on television of us just living in the projects. It's the same impact that, you know, the pimp or the drug dealer used to have.

I feel like a lot of our fashion sensibilities were being taken and being put on the runways of Milan and Paris. I saw an opportunity that it might as well come from us. There were no African-American designers doing that at a mainstream level. And just having the opportunity from all the African-American designers that came before me, and we're breaking down the obstacles and the barriers. Willi Smith, if it wasn't for him, you know, there wouldn't be Rocawear, Sean John, Phat Farm. He was fashion's Martin Luther King. He definitely was inspiring that.

I'd put on a pair of Timberlands and then read in the *Wall Street Journal* that their sales were up, you know, twenty percent. We always use the finest brands to associate ourselves with as a way of us aspiring to be better. But we were having an effect on these brands' bottom line, whether it was Courvoisier or Cristal or Timberland. A lot of these huge companies just started slapping us in the face, whether it was Cristal, saying they didn't want black people drinking their stuff, or Timberland saying that they don't make boots for black people. And so we just started making our own boots.

Hip-hop was a forgotten generation. It was like a generation that really didn't have any parents, and no guidance, and just did the best that we could to survive. The school music programs were cut. We didn't know

SEAN COMBS

how to make any music. Hip-hop is one big family. We were all abandoned and left with each other, so we just created our own world. Everything that's negative in hip-hop, it gets magnified. See, when I lost Biggie, it was something that I had witnessed before, just growing up in the inner city. My father was killed by a gun. All of my best friends were killed by guns. And it's something that has gone on in our world, that has affected, you know, so many of us. I lost Biggie. It was something, sad to say, that I was used to.

To be honest, I didn't understand the importance of family until I got older. When I was growing up, I was brought up by my grandmother and my mother. My father was killed when I was three years old, and I understood the importance of having a mother and a grandmother. It took me time when I had a kid to really understand how to cope with having a big family, because growing up just with my mother and my grandmother and my sister, I was kind of sheltered around women. I understood the aspects of having a big family, and also the importance of it as I went through my trials and tribulations later on in life. I went through so many different traumatic times. And that's when they were there. That's my family. You know, I understood the value of family, 'cause they came to my rescue every time I was in trouble.

> HIP-HOP WAS A FORGOTTEN GENERATION. IT WAS LIKE A GENERATION THAT REALLY DIDN'T HAVE ANY PARENTS, AND NO GUIDANCE, AND JUST DID THE BEST THAT WE COULD TO SURVIVE.

Going to Howard was a culture shock for me, because I'm like one of those true New Yorkers, I didn't really think that, you know, anything else existed besides New York. I didn't understand the many shades and different diversities from around the United States and around the world. And so when I got to Howard, I kind of started to build my global vision of understanding that there were so many different types of people, and people from the South, and the West Coast, and people from Africa and people from London. We're tied together but we have these subtle differences in the things that we like. It was a great education for me, and it helped me in the future as a businessman and also as a producer. It helped me to understand when I was making music or designing clothes that I wanted to do it in such a way that it broke down those differences. That there was an emotional connection that united everybody. And in music, I did it through making music that made people dance, realizing that there was an opportunity out there, that people all over the world wanted to feel good and wanted to dance again.

This was coming off of an era of gangsta rap and it was a time that people really wanted and needed celebration. And that's when I started making my biggest hit records. And I remember being in the studio and thinking back to the times at Howard University and being on the yard and visualizing how my music would make them move and make them feel, and all the different parts of the worlds that they came from.

SUSAN RICE

ASSISTANT SECRETARY OF STATE,
1997–2001
SENIOR CAMPAIGN ADVISER,
BARACK OBAMA 2008
RHODES SCHOLAR

CECIL RHODES, THE man who founded the Rhodes scholarship, wasn't ready for black folks or for women. So when he wrote his will, there weren't supposed to be any of us in there. Alain Locke, the first black Rhodes scholar, in 1907, he snuck in; nobody was supposed to know he was black. We just celebrated his centennial of getting a Rhodes scholarship. In 1976 the British had to pass an act of Parliament for women to be able to be

Washington, D.C., December 10, 2007

eligible for the Rhodes scholarship. So there was a little bit of irony in there. Oh, the other thing I did—with no small touch of irony—was to write my dissertation on Zimbabwe. I used Rhodes's money to go back to Zimbabwe and do my research on how Zimbabwe became independent, and the role that the Commonwealth played in the transition of Rhodesia to Zimbabwe. It gave me a great deal of pleasure to go around and tip liberally with his money all over Zimbabwe.

When I started at the State Department, I was thirty-two years old. I was African-American, I was a noncareer officer, I was a woman, and I was the mother of a three-month-old infant whom I was breast-feeding. And I don't think they'd seen that for a while, if ever. I could only do my best and bring to the game who I was, and other people were going to have to adjust to that. There was no way for me to adjust to their preconceptions.

There was a long-serving and distinguished cadre of senior African-Americans who, for the most part, had made their career in positions on the African continent. Many of them became mentors, people I admire enormously. But among those of us who were political appointees who came at the privilege of the president, we were very few and far between. There have been some obvious leaders—Colin Powell, Condoleezza Rice—but you look down the line, and there are very few African-Americans coming up in the political sphere who are expert in foreign policy.

First of all, it's a field in which for many years there haven't been enough role models, and people haven't seen it as a path that's possible. Now, perhaps with two African-American secretaries of state back to back, young people will start to look at the field differently and see that there is a way forward—and hopefully they won't all be Republican! We Democrats have to do better. It's hard to do what I was fortunate to do; it's hard to come in as a political person. It involves a great deal of luck, on top of some experience and skill. George W. Bush needed Colin Powell badly, and Colin Powell's a great American to have served in those circumstances and put up with what he did. I don't think I could have done that, and I don't think they ever gave him the honor and the credit he was due. He stood in there and had to fight with Rumsfeld and fight with Cheney in a way that arguably was beneath him.

In 1988, Michael Dukakis ran against George Bush. There was a lot of ugliness and racism in that campaign. The Willie Horton ads run against Dukakis were despicable, aimed at sort of surfacing all of the tensions and fears that were still very, very prevalent, and still are. The Bush ads brought that right to the surface. And it came in a context—as you might recall—where, in '88, Jesse Jackson had run a very successful campaign in that context. There was a lot of tension within the Democratic Party about what role Jackson would play in the general election if he wasn't the nominee. Finally, he and his people were brought in, in a quasi-meaningful role. Although I'm sure he and many of us felt not meaningful enough. But then Willie Horton came along just to put fuel on the fire. It was an ugly time. It was just sinister, and it made you angry. It made you feel that we had not come very far from the 1960s, where those sorts of images were used to terrorize and polarize people.

IT'S "OLD THINK," I THINK, TO ASSUME THAT WHAT'S GOOD FOR AFRICAN-AMERICANS IS THE OPPOSITE OF WHAT'S GOOD FOR WHITE FOLKS.

Maybe it's because I work in International Relations and I have a background and an interest in Africa, but I'm struck by how many young people are increasingly interested in Africa. I've got kids coming into my office all the time—black, white, Asian—who are fascinated by Africa. They're studying it in school, they're traveling there, they want to make their careers around things to do with Africa. So, that strikes me as new. Now, maybe I'm looking at a small sample size, but they weren't coming to me ten years ago. There wasn't the same level of interest and attention. And I think when I was coming out of school, the anti-Apartheid movement was very active. That galvanized a lot of us to get interested in Africa. It was important to me. Darfur and, to a lesser extent, the aftermath of Rwanda and Congo, have drawn people's attention to Africa—young people. And now, I think there is reason to be hopeful that, more and more, a more diverse group of young people will look at Africa as a place they want to invest their intellectual energy and their professional skills. So, I'm not pessimistic on that score.

The genocide in Rwanda happened in June of '94. I went in December, part of a U.S. Government delegation. We visited a number of African countries. But my most powerful and searing memory was going to Rwanda

SUSAN RICE

and walking through a churchyard and school where a massive massacre had occurred. And all of the bodies were just where they were the day they were killed—hundreds, if not over a thousand, rotting corpses. I had never seen anything like that before. You're stepping over bodies. I couldn't speak for many hours after that.

American politicians don't talk enough about poverty, domestically or internationally. I think that in the 1960s, when we had Robert Kennedy  and Martin Luther King and even Lyndon Johnson building political platforms around the issue of poverty, it gained a salience that it hasn't achieved since. And perhaps politicians have become fearful of the kinds of solutions that are necessary to deal effectively with poverty. That's a tragedy, because thirty-seven million Americans continue to live in poverty in the richest country in the world. And globally, half the world's population lives on less than two dollars a day! Think about that. You know, you can buy seven pairs of sneakers in this country for what they live on in a year. And somehow, we're not supposed to care.

I'm not sure what Andy Young was thinking when he said that Barack Obama is as black as Bill Clinton. Bill Clinton was a great president of the United States and is a wonderful human being. But he's a white boy from Hope, Arkansas. That is not the same thing as growing up black in America. It diminishes the African-American experience when our leadership does it. We're going to talk about who's black enough and who's dated how many black women!? That is not how we ought to be carrying on our political discourse. It's "old think," I think, to assume that what's good for African-Americans is the opposite of what's good for white folks. Why do we have to have that zero-sum mentality at this point? Why can't we *all* get better health care and better education?

I was born and raised here in Washington, D.C. I went to private schools associated with the Washington National Cathedral, a private coed elementary school that went up to third grade. And then, the National Cathedral School for Girls, which was an elite, predominantly white girls' school here in Washington. I had a phenomenal education, great teachers, good friends, but it was a complicated experience. There was always a little nagging something, and the nagging something was not from the kids that I want to school with, but from some of their parents who, I felt, were telling their daughters, "She's going to get into all these good colleges, and don't you worry about it, she's going to get in 'cause she's black!" There was this subtext of discounting or diminishing my accomplishments. I got mad about that, but I also got motivated by that. My parents always taught me to do my best. Things that make me mad are when it's unfair for others. And I guess that since I was very little, issues of social justice and fairness and equality and opportunity—whether domestically or internationally—have been things that motivate me enormously. I believe that we can do better, and that we are all inherently good and equal, and we need to unleash the opportunity for that equality to be manifest. And so, when I get angry, it's easy for me to channel it into just doing more and doing it harder, and trying to do it better.

SUSAN RICE

CHRIS ROCK

COMEDIAN

PRODUCER

DIRECTOR

THE BLACK LIST? Isn't the Black List people on a list that don't work anymore? Well, the blacklist essentially is that. When they made this list of people that didn't work in the fifties, they essentially treated them as if they were black. I mean, that's pretty much what happened. We're gonna treat you like every black person not named Sidney Poitier. That's what happened. You get treated like black people.

Los Angeles, September 12, 2007

There's progress being made. You know, they have two black women on *The View* now. That's amazing when you really think about it. Because normally, if they're casting a movie, and there's an ensemble, and let's just say they cast, you know, Martin Lawrence or Mos Def or something—I pretty much know they're not gonna hire another black guy. You pretty much know that's it in the ensemble. It's kind of Rat Pack rules: Sammy's in, it's closed. The way I look at the two black women on *The View* is, they actually hired who they thought were the best people for the job and didn't go, "Hey, we already got one black person," and assume that this one black person would represent, you know, if you get one, you got them all.

Oh, you're always black; it's just, what shade of black are you? I don't mean that in an aesthetic way. And there's always gonna kind of be an over-

reaction one way or the other regarding your presence. I always say there's nothing quicker than white praise or white scorn; they come in rapid, and they're boffo reactions. Barack Obama, who's a great candidate who I actually endorse, says four words at a convention. *"He's the greatest man of all time!"* Not really deserved, right? Michael Vick, same thing: The dog thing is bad, but he's the *devil*. I actually saw a guy on TV compare Michael Vick to Mike Tyson goin' to jail. Mike Tyson raped a woman, you know? Hey, I have a dog too. I have daughters too. Guess what? You wanna rape my dog, go right ahead. Just leave my daughters alone, 'cause I'll kill you. And guess what? I've known my dog longer than I've known my daughters. You can still rape my dog.

I've been very fortunate to have some very nice things said about me. But I don't think that's a reflection of the people in the seats. I think I put people in the seats same as Pryor, or Murphy, or whatever, which had nothin' to do with the critics, for the most part. I'm sure I probably made more money doing my first studio movie than Eddie Murphy. Am I better than Eddie Murphy? And Dave Chappelle got fifty million to do his sketch show. I had a sketch show a few years before that. Very similar. But, you know, whoever's next is always gonna have an easier go at it. I've been able to reap the rewards of not only *my* work, but Richard Pryor's work, Bill Cosby's work, Eddie Murphy's work.

The black audience is always gonna be skeptical of anything that white people love: "This can't be that good. White people love it!" In 1996, my first HBO special, there's no white people in the audience. I would tour year-round and see no white people. Then, HBO, blah, blah, blah. Now it's fifty percent, it's forty percent white. Here's a weird story: I was outside the Comedy Store a couple years ago. And this young black girl—she was probably, you know, twenty-three—comes up to me and goes, "Some friends of mine had to drag me to one of your shows. And I thought it was gonna be corny. And it was the best show I ever saw." And the thing that jumped out at me was, she automatically thought my show wasn't gonna be good. She thought it was gonna be corny.

THE BLACK AUDIENCE IS ALWAYS GONNA BE SKEPTICAL OF ANYTHING THAT WHITE PEOPLE LOVE.

All the first twenty black baseball players were superstars. The first one hundred. Those years were skewed. When you let Jackie Robinson in baseball, that doesn't mean it's equal. Baseball, statistically, isn't equal almost until the seventies. And why do I say the seventies? Because that's when you started to see bad black baseball players. Equality is not in being great. Great black people have always been compensated. Jack Johnson was the heavyweight champion of the world, Louis Armstrong—they were compensated for being great. The true equality is the equality to suck like the white man, you know? That's the true equality. I watch the Oscars. OK, these are the people that made the *good* movies. What about the people that made the *bad* movies? That's most of the industry. I wanna be like that. Not that I wanna be bad. But I want the license to be bad, and come back and learn. That's really Martin Luther King's dream coming true: guys suckin'. There's, like, three, four black people in my neighborhood in Alpine. It's Gary Sheffield, Patrick Ewing, Mary J. Blige, and me. Hall of Famer, Hall of Famer, Greatest R & B Singer of Our Time, Decent Comedian. What's the white man next to me? This dentist. OK? That's America. That's what America is. He didn't invent anything. He's just a dentist. Didn't invent veneers, or bonding, or anything. Just a dentist.

My dad used to say this. You can't beat white people at anything. Never. But you can knock them out. So, like, if you have six, and the white guy has five, he wins. Life is like boxing. And you can't let it go. If you're black, you can't let it go to the judges' decision, 'cause you're gonna lose. No matter how bad you beat this man up. Larry Holmes versus Gerry Cooney is the perfect

CHRIS ROCK

example of life. Larry Holmes beats the shit out of this guy for thirteen rounds. He knocks him out in the thirteenth round. They had to stop the fight. The man is bloody. He's been beaten the whole fight. They go to the judges' scorecards, Larry Holmes is losing the fight. If he didn't knock him out, he would've lost the title. And that is essentially the black experience in a nutshell.

MY DAD USED TO SAY THIS. YOU CAN'T BEAT WHITE PEOPLE AT ANYTHING. NEVER. BUT YOU CAN KNOCK THEM OUT.

If my career had stopped in '96, it's still such a success story from where I came from. I was so happy to be out of Bed-Stuy. I was so happy to not be a busboy anymore. I was so happy to not be makin' minimum wage. I was just really happy not being really poor anymore. When I worked at Red Lobster, when I worked at Odd Lots or Alexander's or the *Daily News*, I wasn't working my way through stand-up. That was my life. And I was working with guys that were grown with families, and we were making seven bucks an hour, or something like that.

Bill Cosby paved the way for anybody doin' somethin' like *Everybody Hates Chris*. If there's no *Fat Albert*, there's no *Everybody Hates Chris*. It's weird. My daughter Lola actually goes to sleep with a little Bill doll. That's so cool, man. Like, how much I love Cosby, and it's like—like, actually, both my daughters sleep with little Bills. So someday somebody'll be sleepin' with little Chris. I have a picture in my office of young Cosby with a fedora and a cigar, as cool as they come. And if you actually read the Richard Pryor book *Pryor Convictions*, every time Cosby shows up in the book, he's actually the coolest guy in the Richard Pryor book.

I think Eddie Murphy changed American acting too, a little bit. I just remember the way black guys used to act in movies before *48 Hrs*. There was a sidekick way of acting that Murphy didn't incorporate. It's hard to explain. There's the Negro Ensemble way of acting. Murph was like one of the first black actors who just—it was kind of Brando, in a sense. It's very Brando, because he just acted like a normal person. It's really subtle. Eddie Murphy revolutionized acting for black actors. And no one says that. In *Beverly Hills Cop*, it was just so effortless. It's almost not acting. Before that, it's very earnest: "I'm representing my race!" And Murph kind of just made it, "Hey, I'm Axel. Here's my badge. What's goin' on?"

That's the other great thing about Murphy. Murphy was probably the first comedian to embrace his age. All the other comedians before Murphy, no matter what age they started at, they tried to be older. So they put on a tux or a suit, and they would try to be forty-three years old. They kind of wanted to be in the Rat Pack or somethin'. Where Murph was like the first guy to just be like, "Hey, I'm really twenty-two. And, you know, I'm gonna be electrifying at twenty-two." So Murph was almost like the first rap star, in a sense. He's got leather. It's very Elvis. Elvis would be the closest thing to that.

I remember I got an offer—and I'm not gonna say from who—but a huge offer to do a show like after Chappelle walked away from his money. Somebody calls me up. "Hey, you wanna get a show like that?" Oh, yeah. They

offered me a ton of money—just an insane amount; more money than I have. And so, OK; let me watch the Chappelle show. I put in season two and put it on. And I was like, "There's no way I will ever do a sketch show again." It was so funny. The next guy to do a sketch show can't be me; it's got to be some young kid that doesn't know any better. I think Katt Williams is that guy right now. You know how I always know a comedian's hot? I go to a family function, and no one's asking about me, they're asking about the new guy. "You know Katt Williams? Man, that Katt Williams is funny." It's hot. Now, what you gonna do with the heat? How many pies you gonna cook? If you work hard, you could get ten pies before this oven's cold. You could get a lot of pies. But you have got to have them pies ready and shove them in the oven, and soon as they're ready, you have got to take them out and put some more pies in there.

See, the thing that black culture's missing, it's not the comedian thing. Somebody'll be that guy. The real question is "When are one of these black girls gonna get their Streisand on?" Streisand wrote and directed, man. That's the real question. When is a black girl gonna get her Streisand on? Stop goin' to the premieres and gettin' your picture taken. Really get in there dirty. You're all smart. You're all smarter than me. I can't wait to see the black woman that really gets her Streisand on. That's gonna be the next level. That's the next Oprah. That's the next Will Smith. The black girl that's like, "I'm really about to set it off. I'm writin' a movie, I'm directin' a movie, I'm starrin' in a movie." I can't wait to meet her. I can't wait to work with her.

CHRIS ROCK

SUZAN-LORI PARKS

PULITZER PRIZE–WINNING PLAYWRIGHT

NOVELIST

MACARTHUR FOUNDATION "GENIUS"
  GRANT WINNER

GOD BLESS YOU, Ntozake Shange. She is one of those warrior women writers who has cleared a lot of brush and paths, laid a lot of roads for a lot of us. Writers, nonwriters, women, men, colored girls, and others. You gotta understand, when I was coming up awhile ago, people like Nikki Giovanni were sisters that I looked to. "When I grow up and become a writer, I want to write with that kind of fire, that kind of brilliance, that kind of unflinching

Los Angeles, October 23, 2007

honesty, that kind of bravery. That kind of flair, that kind of music." Same with Gwendolyn Brooks. It doesn't worry me so much that black folks don't go to the theater maybe as much as they used to, only because I just will continue to write and show the things that I write, and, hopefully, encourage the people in the marketing department to be more effective in getting people into the theater.

A lot of the folks who came to see *Topdog/Underdog* were African-American kids, young folks. Most of them had never really been to a play before. So that was their first experience in the theater. They didn't know to show up at eight o'clock. They thought, Yo, it's like a show, I can come at, like, nine, right? And they were coming in with their cell phones on. It was fantastic, because they were learning how to be in the theater. I will continue to create things that will hopefully be of interest to the community. I will continue to encourage folks to come, but I will also continue to encourage the marketing department of theaters to beat those bushes and find creative ways to get the African-American community into the theater. 'Cause a lot of times I think they're just written off. "Oh, black folks don't come"—forget it. You know. Or, "Black folks will only come to black theater," whatever that means.

What is black theater? I'm encouraging the people to consider that a black play is perhaps a work of theater that invites everyone to the table. A black play isn't, like, a play written by black people, with black people on stage. When I think of the work of the brilliant August Wilson, that's what his theater does. His theater invites everyone to the table. So if we were to look in the dictionary, under *black play* you might see "a play written by a black person." OK, definition number one. "A play with black actors," definition number two, perhaps. "A play that invites everyone to the table": definition number three. "A play that practices radical inclusion": definition number four. So there's more at work than just skin color and themes in black theater.

Yeah, you'll hear people screaming things at the stage. I absolutely love that. But that is a people who do not see a separation between their reality—i.e., the reality of the audience—and the reality of a character on stage. We're in the same room. I gotta tell the brotha that somethin's up, you

> WHAT IS BLACK THEATER? I'M ENCOURAGING THE PEOPLE TO CONSIDER THAT A BLACK PLAY IS PERHAPS A WORK OF THEATER THAT INVITES EVERYONE TO THE TABLE.

154

know. That's very radical dramaturgy, if you really think about it. You get the really radical stuff that happens, often in the black community, where the audience feels that they are an active participant, and they have to say, "Go on, sister. You tell him. You tell him." As if it's happening in their living room. Which is very different and very exciting. We have to mine those riches more and celebrate those riches more. I think a lot of times we forget who we are, you know?

I think it's also an African-American thing. That's just a daring avant-garde thing. The African-American thing. Like Ornette Coleman does; he'll take it out there. Or Charlie Parker; whoa, we're gone. That sort of fearlessness. Because we never lose connection with that emotional undercurrent. And the emotional undercurrent is a river, and the river doesn't always flow where you think it's flowing. It's not always flowing A, B, C, D. It's not always flowing that way. It's often flowing in ways that you have to feel, 'cause it's an underground river. The river of spirits, you know? Women are culturally brought up to recognize those things and to be fearless—more fearless about tangents. We're less fearful of being in the margins, 'cause we *are* in the margins. And if you're an African-American woman, you're in the margins of the margins of the margins of the margins. It's like being off-off-off-off-Broadway, where you can do whatever you need to do to get the job done.

Topdog/Underdog, for me, the play's about this dude who doesn't get along with his brother. It's not about the white-man thing. I think a majority of the population imagines that the first thought out of my mind when I get up in the morning is, Whoa, I'm a black woman. How do I fit into the white world? I'm, like, give me a fuckin' break! I mean, I'm, like, yo! Like, my dog needs to go to the bathroom, or my husband is talkin' to me. You know, basic human stuff.

From my mom and dad, I didn't get a lot of stories about the difficult times. I mean, my dad, career army officer, two tours in Vietnam and one tour in Korea, very rarely talked about his experiences in the war. I remember, when we traveled, when he was reassigned from, say, California to Kentucky, or from Kentucky to North Carolina, he would dress in his army uniform. Why? Because if you dressed in your army uniform, the folks on the road were less likely to kill you. That's how dangerous it was, driving in the sixties.

I think if we were less afraid of our own brilliance and ability and power, we would have a lot fewer problems. I find that we are less willing

to embrace the possibilities of our own brilliance. I'm less concerned about the actions of the Man and more concerned about our own behavior, which is ultimately the only thing we can really do something about. The Man got his feet up on the table. He ain't sweatin' it. 'Cause we got brothers on the corners killin' brothers, and sisters on the corners stabbin' sisters. So the Man got his feet up on his desk, 'cause he has effectively outsourced the hating to the community.

Very good. Brilliant! Brilliant. But look what we're left with.

I don't think African-Americans these days have enough mirroring. You know, a child needs certain mirroring from their parents, so they can learn how to be. I think a people also need mirroring, so we could learn how to be. We don't have enough mirroring going on, and a lot of the so-called role models don't want to be role models. It's a difficult time for black folks these days, I think. We're not getting that mirroring from our leadership, and we need it.

My parents had a difficult—beautiful, but difficult—coming up. My father was from Chicago and grew up very poor. My mom lived in Odessa, Texas, which is west of Fort Worth. Her parents were educated. They weren't poor, but they were of modest means. Her mother was a college graduate, a schoolteacher, her father the same, but they went to the segregated schools. My parents went to Southern University, which is in Baton Rouge, Louisiana, which at that time was a historical black college. There was a feeling that we have to improve ourselves and not spend a lot of time talking about the more difficult times. I think we need to encourage each other that we have more going on. By extension, we will

encourage and educate by continuing to do what it is that we do. I'm not
saying go out on a speaking tour, but just through example. I had inter-
views with folks in cities, and they said, "You know,
we're a little nervous that the entire city of Chicago
will be performing plays written by a black woman for
a whole year. We're kind of nervous." And I was like,
why? "Well, we're just nervous." I was like, "Have you
read the plays?" "Well, we've read some of them." Without really taking
your time to look at the work, there is a preconception of what it's about.
It's about, ooh, some angry black people being mad at white people. Well,
read the fucking work, you know what I'm saying? They need to be educated. Or educate themselves.

I THINK IF WE WERE LESS AFRAID
OF OUR OWN BRILLIANCE AND
ABILITY AND POWER, WE WOULD
HAVE A LOT FEWER PROBLEMS.

SUZAN-LORI PARKS

STEVE STOUTE

RECORD PRODUCER

TALENT MANAGER

WITH NAS, I just saw a brilliant artist—a guy who knew how to write, who knew how to basically write poems—that was around street and urban culture. And I just felt like if I worked with him, I could take his art and put it on a bigger platform so that everyone could share and listen to his genius. His first album basically was obscure. I was at Quincy Jones's house, and we started talkin' about Nas. And he just got up and, like, sprinted. Now,

New York City, September 21, 2007

Quincy's knees ain't so good, man. He came back with a picture; he was with Nas's father [Olu Dara]. He showed me some pictures of them in France in the late sixties. He was tellin' me how talented and how much of an artist Olu was. And it really explained to me, when I saw that photo, where Nas's artistry came from.

When I look back on that period of time when there were all those beefs and everything, it was real, right? It was just accepted. I didn't realize how dangerous it was or actually how negative it was. Now, when you look back on it, you're like, man, it was just music. I can't believe that an art form has had to go through that period of East versus West, or who's better than who. These guys were basically beefing over things that were not necessarily important. But people were dying, and people were gettin' hurt, and people were fearful as a result of that. If there's a couple negative spots around hip-hop, I would say that it was the evolution of that negative "who's better than who" and East Coast versus West Coast nonsense: "How down are you?"

The change really happened, unfortunately, after Biggie's and Tupac's passings. It hit home that anybody could be touched, and it had gone too far. And the media played a big role in inciting it. I don't know if I would say that the music got better. Everybody had more guns than the army and what have you. I guess the lyrical content was unexpected because people were throwin' jabs at people and using that as the new way to garner attention and let everybody know that they're tough. When that becomes entertaining as a sideshow is when you know the music is not necessarily gonna get any better because people start relying on the sideshow and not the music. I coulda told everybody when Janet Jackson showed her breast at the Super Bowl, the album was gonna be terrible.

YOU KNOW, THAT'S THE NEW COMPETITION, RIGHT? WHO'S THE BUSINESSMAN? IT'S NOT NO LONGER WHO'S GOT MORE GUNS.

Now the conversation's more about who has what business. Right, 50 Cent owns a piece of Vitamin Water, which was sold to Coca-Cola. You know, that's the new competition, right? Who's the businessman? It's not no longer who's got more guns. I was at Sony Records at the time when I signed 50 Cent. And he was always very clear what his objectives were and how big he wanted to be. And he was always focused on his business. If you got shot at nine times, what would you be thinking about?

I grew up listenin' to the first Run-D.M.C. I would see LL Cool J at the mall all the time in Queens, see LL Cool J at block parties. Bein' fifteen in '85 and sixteen in '86, that's when the music was just on fire, hot. You meet one guy today; tomorrow, the guy's a superstar. He had somethin'. He had a four-fingered ring. You know, he was important. He was a 'hood superstar overnight.

In '88, '87, I used to look at rock music on MTV. And I would see, you know, Bon Jovi. And I'd see Whitesnake. And I'm like, that was just a complete watered-down version of Bob Dylan and Bruce Springsteen. They weren't real. They were just an interpretation of the real. And that's what I'm seein' right now in rap music, like ring-tone rappers and guys just makin' songs that have nothin' to do with the art form or the culture. If it's popular to set yourself on fire, they'll set themselves on fire. Has nothin' to do with the true value of the culture where the music came from. It was fantastic to grow up in it, '85 to '99, the era of counterculture, the era of "This is our music, we created this, and this is for  us." It's what that era represented. There were small record companies that could get your record on the radio. Mr. Magic and Red Alert, these guys were very important; they were on air at midnight. They were on air at two in the mornin'. You had to stay up to listen to the music. And they'd only take the best music. Guys would do everything to try to get on their radar screen. And it was nothin' but good music comin' outta that.

STEVE STOUTE

RICHARD PARSONS

CHAIRMAN, TIME WARNER

I MET THE GOVERNOR of the state of New York. This is 1970. I was in my senior year at law school up in Albany, New York, and I had an internship at the New York State Assembly. Sometime during the middle of my senior year, they offered me an internship, and I bolted; I started working for Nelson Rockefeller. He kind of flashed into this meeting at which I was present and then left. And then, I think, for whatever reason, he decided that I

New York City, August 8, 2007

should work for him instead of them. As my wife and I were going through the receiving line, he fixed on me and turned to his wife, and said, "This young man's going places." And then, when I'd come to the city on occasion—you know, I'd come down to see the folks or just hang out in the neighborhood—people would say, "Oh, look, there's one of the three black Republicans in all of the city." You know, so you'd get a little jostling down here. But Rockefeller was different. He was Republican, but he was the head of something called the Rockefeller Republicans, which was thought to be fiscally conservative, like many Republicans, but socially progressive.

It was the party of Lincoln. It's only a phenomenon more of the postwar years, after World War II, that the Democrats seemed to become the party of the common man. And the Republicans became the party of landed gentry. That postwar era froze into place what we have today, which is still the Democrats' purporting to be the party of the common man and the Republicans' defending the old guard. Both by family heritage and by personal inclination, Rockefeller had a particular standing in the black community that served him well and served those of us who happened to be African-Americans and who worked for him well. That's the first time I met Jackie Robinson. Jackie Robinson was one of the guys who was in the tent for Nelson. In fact, I remember when Nelson died. I was to fly down to get Daddy King—Martin Luther King Jr.'s father—to come up and preach at Nelson's memorial service, because the family had always had this connection to the African-American community and the causes of justice that made it okay to be Republican, if you were a Rockefeller Republican.

I started out as a lawyer. And I spent some time in government. Then I spent some time as a practicing lawyer, practicing privately here. And then I had a client that was a bank. Ultimately I created a relationship where when the chairman of the bank began to contemplate retirement, he asked me if I would consider learning the business and ultimately taking over. And I did. To my surprise, at that time, there were no other African-Americans who were heading up major banking institutions in the United States.

So you'd go to these big banking conferences and things. Talk about splendid isolation! It was me, myself, and I, in terms of representatives of the African-American community. My explanation is that even the right things sometimes just take time. Because the right thing is not just about what's the right thing morally, or what's the right imperative, it's also having the preparation, the experience, and the skills necessary to step into the right job. We all pretty much started out at the same time. We were all children of what I call "the movement," the civil rights movement, from '54 to '64. You know, from *Brown v. Board of Education* to the culmination of the enactment of the Civil Rights Act in 1964. And so you got the same degrees now as everybody else. And then you get on the train at the first stop. And you have to ride through to the end.

It's interesting. Two things were a part of my upbringing that I don't think most white Americans would relate to as part of their upbringing. One, I cannot tell you the number of times that I was told when I was a kid, "You're gonna have to work twice as hard to get half as far." And two—I remember almost as if it were yesterday—whenever my grandmother would send you out somewhere, she'd say, "Now, remember, you want to be a credit to your race." Now, I don't know many of my white, Anglo-Saxon, Protestant colleagues whose parents sent them off into the day saying, "Be a credit to your race," right? It was as if you were carrying a responsibility, not just for yourself or even your family, but for a whole category of people.

BLACK CULTURE LEADS IN AMERICA. AND BECAUSE AMERICA LEADS IN THE WORLD, BLACK POPULAR CULTURE LEADS IN THE WORLD.

I left my law firm and went to the Dime in 1988. And the world by 1988 was a much different place than it was in 1948 when I was born, in 1958 when I was in fifth grade, or in 1968 when I was in college. By 1988 the jailbreak was on. And so people would ask me, "Well, when did it first occur to you that you could become the CEO of a large, money-centered bank?" I had to deal with that question a lot. And I would say to people, "It actually never occurred to me that I couldn't."

It's not so much that it amuses me to hear the way people in America feel compelled to bring in the notion of ethnicity. It feels very different when you're on the playing field. There are innumerable obstacles that you have to either negotiate around or navigate through. Race being but one of them, and not even the most important. At least that's my observa-

RICHARD PARSONS

tion. America is still wrestling with its heritage of what I'll call "structural racism."

Black culture leads in America. And because America leads in the world, black popular culture leads in the world. We have tended, historically, to be on one side of the camera: performing. But when you looked behind the camera to who is determining what stories get told, there you found the real dearth of black Americans. I think that's changing now. Not only will you see African-Americans and other minorities in front of cameras, portraying roles in movies and on television and other mediums, but determining from behind the camera what stories get told, how they get told, on what mediums, where the funding goes. And so there's an increasing balance to the flow of the medium.

DO I FEEL LIKE I'M JUDGED AS A BLACK MAN? THE ANSWER IS, OBVIOUSLY, YES, BECAUSE THIS IS AMERICA.

Do I feel like I'm judged as a black man? The answer is, obviously, yes, because this is America. If you're African-American, you're gonna be judged on either side of the line. If you succeed, "Ah, here's a black person who succeeded." And if you fail, it's like, "Well, here's another black person that failed." And so, we'll know we've made real progress when you just get to be a person.

When I was a kid, I burnt my house down. I mean, like, to the ground. It was an accident. My father and my mother stayed here in New York because he had a job here. But myself and my three siblings, two sisters and a brother, were dispatched to live with my grandmother until the house could be rebuilt. And my grandmother used to sort of sit me in her lap so she could keep an eye on me, right? So I wouldn't burn *her* house down. She read to me from the Bible. Probably the thing that I remember most—I think it's Galatians, chapter six or seven—"Be not deceived. The Lord is not mocked. Whatsoever a man soweth, so also shall he reap." That made an impression on me, but I didn't quite know what it meant. But as I got older and older, and as I watched the way the world works, it's just remarkable to me that that seems to be just so. It's true.

I can remember having these, I'll call them "spirited," conversations with a woman who has since gone to her reward named C. Dolores Tucker. She had a point of view, you know? She thought that some of the music that was coming out of the early to mid-nineties, in terms of the first rap artists and the harsh street and thug sounds and, to some extent, misogynistic sounds, was inappropriate and should be stopped.

And then you'd talk to the artists, who would say, "I'm just depicting what I see out here. And these are protest songs." And the language was raw. And the imagery was raw. But it got down to a discussion about black culture. And about what's appropriate to reflect to the broader culture, what's going on in the black community. And it was quite, I thought, challenging. In fact, I think some of the hardest decisions you had to make

were in that area. For art to grow, for culture to grow, one's reach always has to exceed one's grasp. But what should be outside of even your reach? What should be on the other side of appropriate and constructive? Those debates and discussions both uniquely involved African-Americans, because their culture was leading.

RICHARD PARSONS

DAWN STALEY

THREE-TIME OLYMPIC GOLD MEDALIST

WNBA ALL-STAR

HEAD COACH, TEMPLE UNIVERSITY OWLS

I CAN REMEMBER playing, maybe when I was around six or seven, and it was just a neighborhood thing to do. And it wasn't just basketball. I played tackle football. I played baseball. It didn't matter what I was playing, as long as I was able to go out and compete, and I just had this competitiveness in me, growing up the youngest of five children. I had to fight for virtually every single thing in the household. I realized that in order for me to play

Philadelphia, December 7, 2007

on the big-boy court, you had to pass the basketball, because everybody else wanted to shoot the ball. I knew my niche would be passing the basketball, because of my height and my stature and the fact that I was a girl playing in an all-boy sport. That's when I knew that I had something special, because I started receiving letters from colleges seeking interest in me as a basketball player. There weren't any prominent female role models that I could see, touch, hear. I was just really into what I considered the best. And

that was players in the NBA because I thought they were the best, and in order for me to be best, I like to emulate the best. I didn't really look at the gender.

In the projects in North Philadelphia, Hank Gathers is a playground legend. We grew up in the same housing projects, and I wasn't fortunate enough to play with Hank, because he played on the big-boy court. Once my mom found out that I was on the courts at two in the morning, she just let me go. My father, on the other hand, was pretty skeptical of me just always playing with the guys. And I never was playing with the girls. Actually, the times I did play with the girls, I found myself getting into fights. If I'm playing with one of the girls' boyfriends, maybe she thinks more than basketball is going on. But that was the furthest from my mind. I wanted to play basketball. I wanted to win.

You know, when I was named the player of the year by *USA Today*, I had no idea. So when they called, it was like a boxer being hit by a body blow, and I didn't brace myself for it. I mean, it came out of nowhere. Partly because I grew up in North Philadelphia, and a lot of people don't come to North Philly to see what kind of talent pool that's in there. You have to understand, when you're growing up in the projects, you find things to do at two o'clock in the morning. There were basketball courts in the big field, and any summer night I was in one of those fields, more than likely it was basketball. I would tell my mother that's where I'm going to be, you know, two o'clock in the morning. A lot of times she didn't believe me, but you could see the basketball court from my house. So she would come out and kind of just peek out to see if I was really out there with the guys, playing. And I was. So that's when she started embracing the fact that I could play the game, and I was safe out there. She wasn't always OK with it, having her baby play with the guys so much. But once she found out this is the thing that makes me happy, she was OK with it.

I played in Italy, Spain. I went to Brazil. I went to France. And being an African-American, or just an American in general, I found that it was somewhat difficult. You're stared at no matter where you are. You're stared at on the basketball court. If you're going to the grocery store to pick up some groceries, you're stared at. I think a lot of it is because they haven't seen a black person walk down the street nor live in the same neighborhood as them.

I was able to just hone my skills in my neighborhood, to be creative in it. I butted heads with all of my coaches, to be quite honest, and that's just a part of me wanting to learn. I was a North Philadelphia kid. Going to the University of Virginia, I wasn't used to conforming to the ways in which they did things at Virginia, at a higher-education school. I wasn't used to white people. That's just the nature of where I grew up; if I want something, I'll go get it. If I want something, I'll work to get it. I wasn't used to asking politely and being turned down.

> I BUTTED HEADS WITH ALL OF MY COACHES, TO BE QUITE HONEST, AND THAT'S JUST A PART OF ME WANTING TO LEARN.

Definitely in the WNBA, I just think that players should be able to express themselves as they see fit. I don't see the point of a rule to say you come to the game dressed this way or that way, especially when they're not flying commercially; they charter flights. No one's really going to see them in the locker room and leaving the locker room. No fans, anyway. So, you know, there is some conformity that I disagreed with. I think you should be allowed to be expressive in how you want to dress, or whatever.

On the court, I think the NBA is more individual, and they take advantage of different one-on-one, or two-on-two situations. The WNBA was more like college, where everybody touches the basketball, and it was really fluid. I think nowadays WNBA is moving toward the NBA, where you just have really talented players who have great one-on-one skills, and you want to take advantage of that. I also think that the locker room is moving more toward the NBA; I think we're losing a little bit of what got us here, the reputation of being a team-oriented sport.

To be able to continue to play in the WNBA, to continue to head the

DAWN STALEY

Temple women's basketball team, to play in the Olympics, and represent my country, you don't really dream about doing all those things at once. If you're able to fit all these things in, God bless you. It comes at a price, sacrificing your family, sometimes your social life. All those things took a backseat to my career, but I don't have any regrets. I didn't have a husband, I didn't have children, so I was able to just dive into my profession. And if I had to do it again, I would probably do the same thing.

When I was at Virginia, there was this one incident, in which a twelve-year-old was standing on the roof of this building. I was having a meal at the cafeteria, and we get this call saying that this young lady was about to commit suicide. The only person she wanted to talk to was me, and I'm just shocked. At that time, I did have a reputation of being a very good basketball player. But it really put things in perspective. Because you really don't think you have an influence on a life-or-death situation. She just wanted somebody to let her be the focal point of that particular moment. And sometimes we tend to forget, during our busy day, saying hi to somebody or smiling at somebody could change their outlook on life.

WHAT WOULD MY LIFE HAVE BEEN LIKE WITHOUT BASKETBALL? I WOULD PROBABLY HAVE BEEN A STATISTIC.

What would my life have been like without basketball? I would probably have been a statistic. Just growing up, and seeing how some of the people I grew up with, how they live today—how they *don't* live today. Some of them have been killed. I prioritized basketball, and it was probably the best decision that I made thus far. I think that African-American women are very powerful people, and to be an athlete, it's added pressure. But you got these kids over here who are in desperate need of hope. Someday you can provide them with the tools in order for them to be successful, and that's what I try to do. I think I, as an African-American woman, athlete, daughter, friend, I could make a difference in the world, just because I excelled at playing a sport, excelled at a passion. That's the beautiful thing.

Since I retired, I've had an opportunity to just reflect on what I was able to accomplish. Not just from a basketball standpoint, but from a neighborhood standpoint. I still go to the neighborhood I grew up in just to hear the people and wave and say hello, that's what makes me proud. They know more about what I'm doing than probably I do.

They followed me from Dobbins, to Virginia, to playing overseas, to playing in the Olympics, to coaching at Temple. I think everything comes full circle at some point. I chose to go to college outside of my hometown. I think

it's good for people to venture out a little bit. And I think it's also great to come back. I don't think I could have gotten into coaching in any other city. Temple was the perfect place for my mentality. It's north Philadelphia, not a place that a lot of people would think you could get a great education, great basketball. And that's my thing.

COLIN POWELL

U.S. SECRETARY OF STATE, 2001–2004

CHAIRMAN OF THE JOINT CHIEFS OF STAFF,

1989–1992

I HAD NEVER been in the South until I started my army career in 1957 in ROTC summer camp. My poor father saw me off at the bus station in Manhattan, thinking he'd never see his son alive again. But the army had already moved into integration and desegregation at the time I came along. I could compete with the kids from Duke University or North Carolina University. And I didn't feel the least bit inferior, because I was raised not to

Washington, D.C., December 11, 2007

feel inferior. I took full advantage of the opportunities that were created for African-Americans after the Civil Rights Act of '64 and the Voting Rights Act of '65. It was in 1948 that Truman signed the desegregation order. He signed an order. They didn't take it to Congress to pass a law. No law integrating the army would have passed the Congress in 1948. So Truman just signed an order and said do it. It took another five years for it to happen. It didn't happen overnight. There was resistance in the military. I came into the army five years after that, 1958.

> NO LAW INTEGRATING THE ARMY WOULD HAVE PASSED THE CONGRESS IN 1948. SO TRUMAN JUST SIGNED AN ORDER AND SAID DO IT. IT TOOK ANOTHER FIVE YEARS FOR IT TO HAPPEN.

Very often I've been given assignments that were good assignments, and people said, "Well, you know why Powell got that job. They needed a black guy." And my answer to that, when I hear these rumors coming back, I just smile and say, well, fine; for two hundred years, I didn't get the job because they needed all whites. So I'm not going to argue about that. The only thing that's going to count now is my performance.

You know, one of the most difficult times in my career was when I was chairman of the Joint Chiefs of Staff, and we had the riots in Los Angeles in 1992. For me to have to send troops at the direction of the president to Los Angeles to put down this riot was distasteful. But it had to be done. We had to bring order back to the streets of Los Angeles. But I commented then that I thought it was terribly disturbing to me as a black man—and it should be disturbing to all Americans—that Rodney King was treated in such a manner. I thought that I should say that out loud to make sure that nobody had any question that an injustice was done. So the riot had to be brought to an end. The cause of the riot, what happened to Rodney King, had to be dealt with. And we had to make sure things like that did not continue to happen in America.

Back in 1964, it wasn't hard to make a choice between Barry Goldwater and Lyndon Johnson, who was committed to civil rights, and Goldwater who was not. Being a black soldier in Fort Benning, Georgia, with your wife in Birmingham, Alabama, in 1964, and driving a Volkswagen—one of them *"furren cars"* with a New York State license plate on it, and an LBJ sticker—was a chancy thing to do. And once I got stopped—speeding, no doubt, from Birmingham back to Fort Benning, Georgia, somewhere around Silicog, Alabama. I pulled over to the side of the road. The state trooper came along. I could see him in my rearview mirror as he approached: clomp, clomp, clomp, clomp. Knee-high boots. Brown hat. And he looked down at me, this black man sitting behind the wheel of this Volkswagen. And he said, "Hmm, foreign car. New York license plates. LBJ sticker. Boy, you need to get out of here as fast as you can!" And I drove off. One of the kindest things ever done to me.

My favorite part of *Purlie Victorious,* the musical, is at the very end. The story of *Purlie Victorious* is, the Reverend Purlie goes in and saves the black church down South from racist Old Cap'n. And at the end of the play,

Purlie now has to move on. Reverend Purlie has to go save someone else, somewhere else. And the people are saying, "Stay here, Purlie! Stay here!" And he says, "No, I must go." He says, "But before I go, I want to say this to you: Let the Declaration of Independence inspire you, let the Constitution of the United States protect you. And do what you can for the white folks." And so, the beauty of that was—I may not have got the lines exactly right—but the last line

is right. Do you what you can for the white folks. And I've never forgotten that, because what he was saying is there are a lot of white folks in America who still have not crossed over and realized that black people and Hispanics and all others should be judged solely on performance and not the color of the skin, or their background, or the accent of their language. And that's what Dr. Martin Luther King did so effectively. He didn't just lead blacks. He did what he could for the white folks. By taking a mirror and holding it up so that white people could look into that mirror and see what was going on in America. I've always remembered that line from *Purlie Victorious* and traced it back to what Dr. King was trying to do. And what I've tried to do in my career.

Purlie Victorious captured America at a time when blacks had to play this secondary role even when they were smarter than their white masters. They could not show it. It was always "Yowsa," "yessuh." Even though they were laughing behind Master's back because they knew more than he did.

COLIN POWELL

We had to play this role for so many hundreds of years. And then Purlie comes along and shakes up the system.

My profession in the military, it was the same way. Can blacks actually be soldiers? One of my favorite stories is of a Civil War Confederate general who heard that the president of the Confederacy, Jefferson Davis, was going to start recruiting black men into the Confederate Army. And he wrote him and said, "Don't do this! You can't do this! Use Negroes for whatever purpose you want: chopping wood, digging trenches, hauling cargo. But you can't make them soldiers. Because if a black man can carry a rifle and defend the South just like a white man, then our whole theory of slavery

is wrong, and we will fail." And we knew that. And this general knew that. And we demonstrated our valor. And sooner or later, we prevailed.

A man who is a leading candidate for president of the United States now is on stage with the most famous celebrity in all of America. And they're both black. And when I talk to my children and my grandchildren, they just see this as normal. I've had some interviewers say to me, why do you linger on this? I mean, it's all over. It isn't all over. It's not all over. It can't be all over as long as we have young African-American boys and girls who are not able to get the quality education they need. So there are lots of African-Americans who have succeeded in life, and that's great. But we should not think that this second Civil War is over until we have provided opportunities for all Americans: African-Americans, Hispanic Americans, poor white Americans.

I have to say I know lots of black Americans who did not have West Indian parents, but had that same background that gave them the strength and resiliency to do well in American society. But I think those of us of immigrant West Indian heritage probably had a little more of an advantage than most of my African-American brothers and sisters who were native born, in that my parents came to the country with a British tradition—commitment to education, the strength of the family. I like to tell the joke that when I was growing up in the South Bronx section of New York, I had little choice except to sort of mind my manners and get my education, even though I wasn't very good at it. Because in every other apartment building in the South Bronx, one of my West Indian aunts lived. And they hung out the window all day long looking down to catch any cousin in any kind of misdemeanor or felony. And they were authorized to do something about it on the spot. You talk about the speed of the Internet today, you should have seen the speed of the Aunt-net in the South Bronx fifty years ago when one of the kids got in trouble. They also told us that we are members of a proud family. And we came here to take advantage of this wonderful country, America.

A MAN WHO IS A LEADING CANDIDATE FOR PRESIDENT OF THE UNITED STATES NOW IS ON STAGE WITH THE MOST FAMOUS CELEBRITY IN ALL OF AMERICA. AND THEY'RE BOTH BLACK. AND WHEN I TALK TO MY CHILDREN AND MY GRANDCHILDREN, THEY JUST SEE THIS AS NORMAL.

COLIN POWELL

BILL T. JONES

DANCER
TONY AWARD WINNER
DIRECTOR, BILL T. JONES/ARNIE ZANE
  DANCE COMPANY

NOW, HERE YOU are talking to a black man of a certain age, and we were taught that we're supposed to be a lot of things, but we're supposed to be fearless, right? Well, I suppose I guess we're past that, aren't we? You know, Arnie Zane, my companion, this Jewish-Italian man that I fell in love with, he had a kind of fearlessness that came with maybe being a sexual out-law. I remember once—he knew how to get to me—we were young guys in

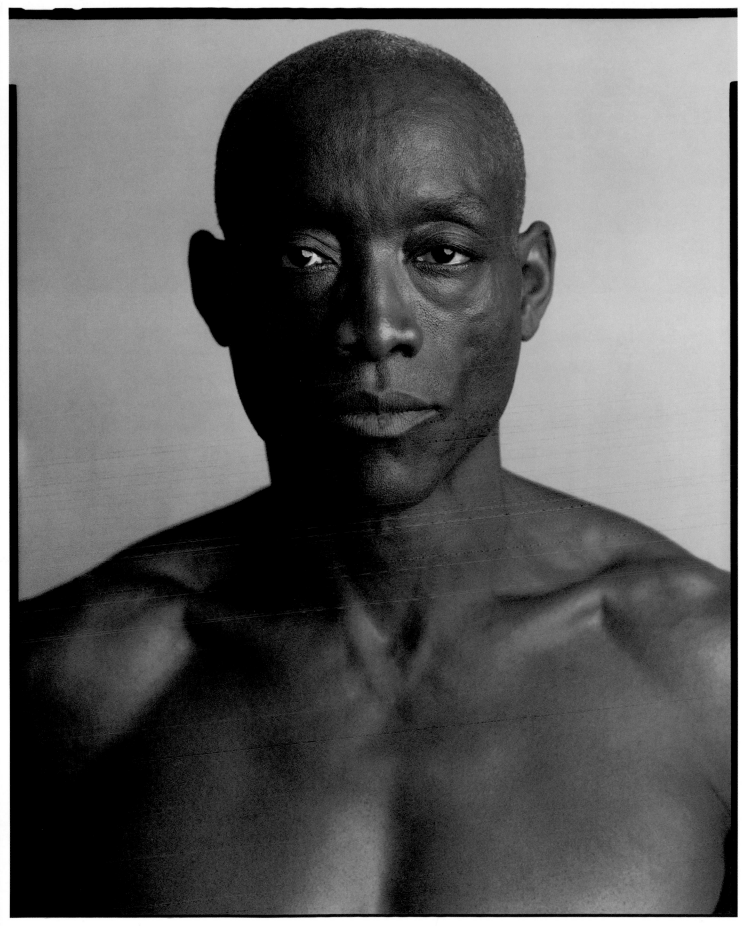

New York City, September 20, 2007

upstate New York, shopping at thrift stores and trying to live the revolution, walking down the street holding hands and all that. And then certain things he would wear: padded shoulders, Joan Crawford. And he said, "If you were a liberated man, you wouldn't be concerned."

"What, liberated? You know, Estella Jones was my mother! Civil rights! What do you mean, liberated?"

And he looked me right in the eye, and he said, "No, you're afraid; you're afraid that people will call you a freak."

I think that maybe I went too far. There was this idea that you had to be in the face of the world. Now, the dance world, the genteel world of modernism and abstraction, did not understand what this heat was about.

"Whoa, young man, we're your friends—why are you so angry? What's the problem?"

I felt somewhat concerned when *Time* magazine referred to me as America's foremost black choreographer, but I have so many battle scars. Let me tell you a story about being at the Brooklyn Academy of Music one morning that made battle lines that I'm still dealing with today. It was called *The Future of Black Dance*. Well, I was on the stage with the likes of Carmen de Lavallade, Tally Beatty, George Fason—an interesting group of theater workers—and I said at one point (I was reading Proust at the time), "I feel that I'm an artist first, and then I'm black. I feel that my work could be a description of the space between two clouds." You know, thinking about Proust and *Within a Budding Grove*. The room exploded. The room exploded! Because this person denied his blackness. I thought that's what a modernist artist was supposed to do: break out of categories. And I was a product of the sixties; we are not our bodies, all that stuff. Well, I got a lesson that day. So, to have them years later, fast forward, and now the "mass media" has discovered you, and they're going to put that label on you, that was ironic.

There's so much conservatism in the black community. I feel that I have been on so many sides of this issue. The whole notion of identity politics—which seem to have congealed in the minds of academics somewhere circa 1985 and reached its peak maybe by 1995—I was oftentimes used as a poster boy for that. So, my identity, all the titles that you associate with my brand, were very useful to academia, and very useful in a way in the cultural discourse when you want to talk about what in the sixties was called black rage. Now it's called the alienation of people with color, or what have you. Blacks as being conservative has to kind of grate on the notion of blacks as being the hip class, the class that gave us the pot-smoking Louis Armstrong, the supercool Miles Davis, and Muhammad Ali. "Float like a butterfly, sting like a bee"? It's lonely out here if you don't have that community that defines you. So the conservatism is something that any working artist or intellectual has to understand; when is it important and when do you take issue with it? While working on *Uncle Tom's Cabin,* I had to say to my white friends in the avant-garde, "You don't understand why I use religious references," because, quite frankly, look at who our political leaders have often been: Reverend Martin Luther King, Reverend Jesse Jackson, Reverend Al Sharpton.

Years ago at a groovy dinner that was part of SITE Santa Fe, I was with Thelma Golden and Sherrie Levine and some other people, and Sherrie Levine was remarking, "Wow, we've got four black people at the table!" Now, this is an art world event. At that moment, I thought, Oh my God, what is this? What world do I live in that this is unusual?

I'm not sure anymore about this idea of selling out. When I look at the *New York Times* today, it's Kanye West and 50 Cent: Whose CD is going to sell the most? Who's going to sell the most CDs? And this is the front page of the Arts section. The amount of ink that our rap stars get around their posturing. What was it Usher said a few years ago? "The man, the music, the mogul." You can't be a successful artist anymore, you've got to be making it big-time. It's like you've got to be slaying the charts everywhere, because then you're a player. You know, one of my gods is James Baldwin. He was a small, elegant, soft man with a razor-sharp mind, speaking the King's English better than most, his references are broad, and yet there was no doubt he was a down brother. So that's what I think is important.

I am always struggling with authenticity. Am I a down brother? Because being a black man of culture means that there's something about it you've got to get over. Remember the lyric, "Trying to get over . . ."? I was

YOU CAN'T BE A SUCCESSFUL ARTIST ANYMORE, YOU'VE GOT TO BE MAKING IT BIG-TIME. IT'S LIKE YOU'VE GOT TO BE SLAYING THE CHARTS EVERYWHERE . . .

BILL T. JONES

trying to explain that concept to a table full of my white friends, and they get uncomfortable with this and look at me like "what do you mean?" Well, the great, dark fear in my life is that there always will be a chasm between me and most people, be they black or white, because of the particularities of how I was raised in the world: speaking two languages, putting forward signals that at once said I'm safe, I'm not going to hurt you; I'm smart, I'm not stupid; you can respect me, and you are not going to hurt me. I felt all of these my whole life. Now, I have had to tame that—where they touch the button, and suddenly I let you know that I'm black and you're not, because, in a way, the society is fatigued with it; it fatigued the art world. Yawn: "Black rage, I'm so bored with it." You know? "Why don't you get over it already? Look at you, you won a Tony Award!" "Look at you, you were on *Time* magazine, what are you complaining about? You're not a welfare mother." This identity came with my upbringing that was not about the black church. I had to appropriate that.

> MY MOTHER'S PRAYERS; MY FATHER'S WIT, HIS STORIES, HIS COOL, HIS CONFIDENCE— THOSE ARE THINGS THEY GAVE ME. I SING MY MOTHER'S SPIRITUALS BECAUSE THAT IS THE HEIRLOOM SHE GAVE ME; SHE COULD GIVE ME NOTHING ELSE.

My mother's prayers; my father's wit, his stories, his cool, his confidence—those are things they gave me. I sing my mother's spirituals because that is the heirloom she gave me; she could give me nothing else. I maybe have a longing for that community. When I do find myself in a church—and being the apostate that I am, I don't go there very often—I weep. And I tried to bring that to the stage. Authenticity. Identity. Love. Faith. Transcendence.

What I've gotten from my mother and father, who were the conduits of black culture for me, what I've gotten from being a working-class person: Is it all there? Is it cooking? You know, one night I was invited to do an evening honoring Nick Ashford and Valerie Simpson up in Harlem. There was a big band on stage, there were a lot of people singing and doing their songs, and Daniel Bernard Romain, a fantastic young violinist, composer, and friend of mine. I said, "Daniel, I want you to study Ashford-Simpson's music and give me some licks."

Well, we came in for the rehearsal that afternoon, and the band was like, "What? What is this? We're doing that?" There was a fight. I said, "Look, I was invited to do this—they were my friends." Well, they let me do it, and that night, man, I killed. That night at this gala, Daniel is on his violin doing

"You're All I Need to Get By," and Bill T. Jones is doing the isolations that he's learned from everywhere, from Trisha Brown to Merce Cunningham to James Brown. It was all there, and it was real. It was groovy, it was hip, it was funky, it was smart, it was generous, and I think it was lovely, considering how the audience responded. Am I black enough? Man, I was black and more that night.

ABOUT THE BLACK LIST

SLASH is the former lead guitarist of Guns N' Roses. As a studio musician, he has recorded with, among others, Alice Cooper, Sammy Hagar, Bad Company, Cheap Trick, Ray Charles, Michael Jackson, and Stevie Wonder.

TONI MORRISON is a novelist, essayist, and critic. A bestselling author, she has been awarded the Nobel Prize for Literature, the Pulitzer Prize, and a Grammy.

KEENEN IVORY WAYANS is an actor, comedian, director, and writer. The creator of the television comedy *In Living Color,* he is active in both film and television.

VERNON JORDAN, a lawyer and business executive, was a close adviser to President William Jefferson Clinton. Jordan was previously president of the United Negro College Fund and was president of the National Urban League.

FAYE WATTLETON is an activist for the rights of women. The first African-American and youngest-ever president of Planned Parenthood, she is currently the president of the Center for the Advancement of Women and also serves on the board of trustees at Columbia University.

MARC MORIAL served as mayor of New Orleans from 1994 to 2002. He is president and CEO of the National Urban League.

SERENA WILLIAMS has been ranked the world's number-one player in women's tennis and has won eight Grand Slam singles titles and an Olympic gold medal in women's doubles.

LOU GOSSETT JR. has worked as an actor for more than a half century. An Emmy and Golden Globe winner, he received the Academy Award for best supporting actor in 1983 for *An Officer and a Gentleman.*

RUSSELL SIMMONS, a pioneer in the world of hip-hop, founded the label Def Jam, which produced albums by the Beastie Boys, LL Cool J, Public Enemy, and Run-D.M.C., among others.

LORNA SIMPSON is an acclaimed artist and photographer. In 2007, the Whitney Museum of American Art held a twenty-year retrospective of her work.

MAHLON DUCKETT began his baseball career in 1940 when he joined the Philadelphia Stars at the age of seventeen. Playing there through 1949, he finished out his career in the Negro League with the Homestead Grays in 1950.

ZANE is a *New York Times* bestselling author of erotic fiction, whose titles include *Love Is Never Painless, The Sex Chronicles*, and *Addicted*. Millions of copies of her books are in print.

AL SHARPTON is a minister and a political and civil rights activist. In 2004, Sharpton ran for the Democratic nomination for the president of the United States.

KAREEM ABDUL-JABBAR played for twenty years in the NBA, from 1969 to 1989. During that time, he scored more points than any other player in league history. He is the bestselling author of seven books, including *Black Profiles in Courage* and *On the Shoulders of Giants*.

WILLIAM RICE was one of the Tuskegee Airmen, the legendary group of all-black pilots who flew with distinction during World War II as the 332nd Fighter Group of the United States Army Air Corps.

THELMA GOLDEN is the director and chief curator of the Studio Museum in Harlem. She has also worked at the Whitney Museum and the Metropolitan Museum of Art.

SEAN COMBS, rapper, record producer, actor, and entrepreneur, is the founder of Bad Boy Records and the Sean John clothing line. A Grammy Award–winning performer, he has also appeared in several films and on Broadway.

SUSAN RICE was the United States assistant secretary of state for African Affairs from 1997 to 2001. She holds degrees from Stanford University and Oxford University, which she attended as a Rhodes Scholar.

CHRIS ROCK is known as a successful comedian, screenwriter, producer, director, and actor. His television work has earned him three Emmy awards and fifteen nominations.

SUZAN-LORI PARKS is a playwright and screenwriter whose 2001 play *Topdog/Underdog* won the Pulitzer Prize for Drama. She is also the recipient of a MacArthur Foundation "Genius" Grant and a Guggenheim Fellowship.

STEVE STOUTE is a recording industry executive and manager who has worked with Nas, Gwen Stefani, Beyoncé Knowles, and Jay-Z.

RICHARD PARSONS is chairman of the board of Time Warner. Prior to joining Time Warner, he was chairman and CEO of the Dime Bank.

DAWN STALEY attended the University of Virginia and led its women's basketball team to four NCAA tournaments. She was named the ACC female athlete of the year and the national player of the year in 1991 and 1992. She played in the WNBA for six years and is currently head coach of the women's basketball program at Temple University.

COLIN POWELL was the United States Secretary of State from 2001 to 2004. He served as National Security Advisor from 1987 to 1999 and as chairman of the Joint Chiefs of Staff from 1989 to 1992.

BILL T. JONES is an internationally celebrated dancer, choreographer, and artistic director. In 1982, he founded the Bill T. Jones/Arnie Zane Dance Company. He has received a Tony Award, a MacArthur Foundation "Genius" Grant, and several fellowships from the National Endowment for the Arts.

ACKNOWLEDGMENTS

First and foremost, this book wouldn't be possible without the reams of hard-won observations, ruminations, and reflections from the twenty-five interview subjects who gave so freely of their time to us. Without them, there wouldn't be a book, a movie, or the excitement that still keeps this project alive. Growing up, I used to read comics titled "Tales to Astonish" and "Tales of Suspense"—apt titles for the adventures of the Marvel superheroes contained therein, and also for the pitched battles that took us from colored and negro to black and African-American, so eloquently and honestly elaborated upon by the people who spoke to us and sat for their portraits. And to show that no good deed goes unpunished, special thanks to Thelma Golden and Toni Morrison; they were the first subjects at a time when this idea was still inchoate. They may have been under the impression—and we have no idea where they might have got this notion, the authors mutter disingenuously—that we were experimenting and didn't plan on keeping them for the final version. Both were so good that we found ourselves shooting live rounds from the outset, rather than blanks.

The teenagers who were initially a pack of businessmen curious about a nascent project kept their eyebrows from full mast just below their hairlines and later became the warriors of what the world now knows as Freemind Ventures, our producing partners on the film: Scott Richman, Michael Sloane, Chris McKee, and Payne Brown. They all leapt aboard with both feet as the craft jerked away from the pier, though their occasional questions could still be heard above the roar of the motors: "Are you guys sure this is the way to do this . . . ?" But their queries were simply those of people who wanted the best for the project—an unabashed investment from them in every sense of the word. For his work in planning and logistics, Tommy Walker—executive producer on the project—pulled things together with such calm deftness that laboring to get *The Black List* finished in roughly four months of real time didn't seem like such an absurd prospect. It's only seeing the book you hold in your hands that makes us realize how insane we were to begin with: kids, please don't try this at home.

Mary Bradley demonstrated the same persistence and charm in securing talent in booking people for *The Black List* that she did in her years of producing *The Treatment*.

Sheila Nevins and Lisa Heller at HBO Documentary Films came through with such enthusiasm and devotion of resources that completing this project didn't seem daunting, but rather a fait accompli. Peter Borland and his team at Atria Books treated us, and *The Black List*, exactly the same way. Such commitment precluded any worry about assembling this book in an insanely abbreviated period. It'll probably take you longer to read it than it did for them to assemble it. Thanks to Judith Curr, Nancy Singer, Philip Bashe, Isolde Sauer, and Nick Simonds. Scott Waxman's eye for detail, which included joining us to Atria, is proof positive that despite what you hear, agents do have souls. Well, this one does, anyway.

Lukas Hauser's acuity wasn't simply limited to editing *The Black List* documentary.

He devised segues, color schemes, and typography that lend graphic vitality not only to the film but the book as well. Maybe he can now go home and get some sleep.

Hiram Butler, Timothy's good friend and Houston gallerist, thought *The Black List* portraits deserved a wide audience. He urged Peter Marzio, director of the Museum of Fine Arts, Houston, and Anne Tucker, its chief photography curator, to view them. They were immediately enthusiastic, arranged an exhibition, and are formulating plans for a tour of the portraits. We are enormously grateful to them and their team, including Mary Haus and Paul Johnson.

At the risk of sounding impossibly corny—and more than likely succeeding—I have to say that I cannot believe this project has come to such a satisfying conclusion. When Timothy invited me to his home just a couple of years ago, dropped a stack of photo books on African-American life onto one of his handsome antique tables, and said, "Why haven't we done something on this?" I wouldn't have imagined that ideas would come flying so quickly. Or that we would end up with a book, a film, a museum show, and finally a process that I will treasure for the rest of my life. I have a lot to thank him for, most importantly for filling a void in my life. I lost a brother as we put *The Black List* in motion; I feel like I have another one now. Welcome to my family, White Chocolate Thunder.

—Elvis Mitchell

Photographers tend to be obsessive record keepers. Along with the actual prints and negatives, their archives tend to include cross-references of subjects' addresses, phone numbers, cellphone numbers, fax numbers, email, agents, PR contacts, food preference, political persuasions, favorite designers, and even favorite music. Some even jot down a memorable note or two about the shoot itself. So I can say for a fact that on February 24, 2005, Toni Morrison was having a lunch break in my kitchen on East 2nd Street. We were shooting portraits that day of Toni, Denyce Graves, Angela Brown, Greg Baker, and Richard Danielpour for Ms. Morrison's upcoming opera, *Margaret Garner.* The conversation turned to "divas" as Toni told us about the many many extraordinarily talented performers she had auditioned for the opera. "We should do a portrait book on these women. We can call it . . . *Black Divas,*" Toni said.

Black Divas got me thinking about all the African-Americans I knew and had photographed, the amazing artists, writers, activists, and generals. I started to make a list: Toni, of course, Thelma Golden, Richard Parsons, Faye Wattleton, Colin Powell, and Bill T. Jones quickly came to mind.

Eventually, I called my friend and neighbor from down the block, Elvis Mitchell. "I think I have a book idea . . . let's have lunch." We went out for Thai food. And was it really a book, or a portrait series? Or maybe a film? By the end of lunch, we had 175 names on napkins.

"Let's call it *The Black List*, Elvis said. "We need to make it a good thing to be on *The Black List.*"

Meetings were taken. People were hired. Film was exposed. Video was shot. Files were archived. Things grew. Friends were made. Footage was edited. Good things happened. And, most important, it was fun.

Thanks are due to the interviewees for their time, their wisdom, and their humor. It was a great honor for me to photograph each of them. Thanks are due, over and over again, to our partners at Freemind Ventures: Michael Sloane, Scott Richman, Chris McKee, and Payne Brown, and to Tommy Walker. Thanks to Lukas Hauser for flawless film editing and for the graphics he designed for the film, the book, the posters, and the website.

At Atria Books, special thanks to our editor, Peter Borland, and our publisher, Judith Curr, as well as to Isolde Sauer, Al Madocs, Nancy Singer, Fausto Bozza, and Nick Simonds who all made valuable contributions.

Finally, thanks to Elvis Mitchell. You never wavered in your vision for *The Black List*. Your belief that this project was special and important gave us all a sense of purpose and mission. Your skills as an interviewer are magical. And just when I started to take your extraordinary abilities for granted, you'd surprise us all with your brilliance and charm. I think you have indeed made it a good thing to be on *The Black List.*

—*Timothy Greenfield-Sanders*